Blue Finance: Building the Sustainable Ocean Economy with Blue Bonds, Debt Swaps, Nature-Positive Finance, Ocean Conservation, and Climate Solutions

Copyright

Blue Finance: Building the Sustainable Ocean Economy with Blue Bonds, Debt Swaps, Nature-Positive Finance, Ocean Conservation, and Climate Solutions

ISBN (eBook): 978-1-991369-95-6

ISBN (Paperback): 978-1-991369-96-3

Published by Global Climate Solutions

First Edition, 2025

Cover design and interior layout by Global Climate Solutions

Table of Contents

Introduction

Chapter 1: Understanding the Blue Economy and the Finance Gap

Chapter 2: Principles and Objectives of Blue Finance

Chapter 3: Blue Bonds as a Mechanism for Ocean Investment

Chapter 4: Debt-for-Nature Swaps and Sovereign Blue Finance

Chapter 5: Public and Multilateral Financial Instruments for Blue Investment

Chapter 6: Private Capital and Blended Finance Models

Chapter 7: Governance, Regulation, and Fiduciary Standards

Chapter 8: Measurement, Impact, and Accountability Frameworks

Chapter 9: Scaling Blue Finance Through Innovation and Policy Alignment

Conclusion

Introduction

Oceans have always inspired awe, providing humanity with a sense of vastness, possibility, and connection. They are the world's largest ecosystem, home to extraordinary biodiversity, a regulator of climate, and the foundation for millions of livelihoods and communities. Yet in the early twenty-first century, the state of our oceans is at a crossroads. Widespread overexploitation, accelerating climate change, loss of critical habitats, pollution, and governance failures have eroded the health of marine and coastal systems, threatening both planetary and human wellbeing. As the urgency to reverse this decline grows, the spotlight is increasingly turning to the role of finance in shaping the future of the blue economy.

This book, *Blue Finance: Building the Sustainable Ocean Economy with Blue Bonds, Debt Swaps, Nature-Positive Finance, Ocean Conservation, and Climate Solutions*, explores how financial innovation and coordinated investment can drive a new era of ocean stewardship. It is a guide for practitioners, policymakers, investors, donors, and community leaders who recognize that traditional approaches to marine management and funding are no longer sufficient. It offers an in-depth examination of the instruments, governance frameworks, measurement systems, and enabling policies required to align financial flows with the sustainable use, restoration, and protection of our oceans.

The Ocean Economy: Opportunities and Risks

The blue economy, comprising sectors such as fisheries, aquaculture, shipping, renewable energy, tourism, and marine biotechnology, has immense potential to support sustainable development and economic growth. According to the OECD, the global ocean economy could double in size by 2030, reaching over $3 trillion and providing hundreds of millions of jobs. However, the benefits of ocean resources are increasingly at risk. Over one-third of global fish stocks are overexploited, coral reefs face existential threats from warming and acidification, and coastal cities are vulnerable to sea-level rise and extreme weather events.

The paradox is stark: while the ocean's contribution to economic and human wellbeing is growing, so too are the pressures undermining its resilience. Addressing this paradox requires bridging the gap between the vast sums invested in extractive or unsustainable activities and the relatively modest resources directed toward conservation, resilience, and regeneration. The World Economic Forum and the United Nations have both highlighted the urgent need to redirect, mobilize, and scale finance to meet global ocean targets, whether under the Sustainable Development Goals (especially SDG 14: Life Below Water), the Paris Agreement, or emerging biodiversity frameworks.

Why Blue Finance Now?

The concept of "blue finance" reflects a profound shift in thinking: it is not enough to rely on public budgets, grants, and philanthropic donations to safeguard the ocean. Instead, a full spectrum of financial instruments, debt and equity, public and private, concessional and commercial, must be marshalled to unlock investment at the scale and speed required. Blue finance refers to the intentional mobilization of capital for projects and activities that deliver measurable benefits for marine ecosystems, climate resilience, and coastal communities.

Recent years have seen encouraging momentum. The world's first sovereign blue bond, issued by the Republic of Seychelles in 2018, showed that innovative financial products could link debt management to marine conservation. Debt-for-nature swaps are now being reimagined to support not just terrestrial but also marine outcomes, particularly in island and coastal states grappling with heavy debt burdens and high climate vulnerability. Development banks, impact investors, and mainstream asset managers are launching new blue funds, while fintech and digital platforms are democratizing access to marine investment and improving transparency.

Yet this progress is still nascent compared to the need. The global investment gap for ocean health remains measured in the hundreds of billions of dollars. Barriers such as fragmented governance, weak project pipelines, uncertain returns, data limitations, and the risk of "blue-washing" continue to impede the flow of capital into genuine ocean solutions.

Purpose and Structure of This Book

Blue Finance is designed to bridge knowledge and action. It provides both the conceptual foundation and practical guidance required to design, deploy, and scale financial solutions for a sustainable ocean economy. The book is organized into nine chapters, each addressing a core dimension of blue finance:

- **Chapter 1** defines the blue economy and analyzes the persistent finance gap undermining ocean sustainability.
- **Chapter 2** articulates the principles and objectives that must guide blue finance, emphasizing additionality, accountability, and alignment with global goals.
- **Chapter 3** explores blue bonds, their structure, design, and unique potential to channel capital to marine projects.
- **Chapter 4** examines debt-for-nature swaps and the tools available to sovereigns seeking to link fiscal stability with environmental ambition.
- **Chapter 5** reviews the critical role of public and multilateral finance, including grants, concessional loans, guarantees, and results-based approaches.
- **Chapter 6** details the emergence of private capital and blended finance, unpacking how risk-sharing and innovation can attract new investors.
- **Chapter 7** surveys the governance, legal, regulatory, and fiduciary frameworks that underpin the integrity of blue finance.

- **Chapter 8** focuses on measurement, impact, and accountability, with an emphasis on robust metrics, verification, and community outcomes.
- **Chapter 9** considers how innovation and policy alignment can scale blue finance, from digital tools to national strategies and the mainstreaming of ocean-positive investment.

Throughout, the book addresses both the enabling conditions and persistent barriers faced by governments, financiers, project developers, and communities. It draws on the latest research, standards, and emerging best practices, while acknowledging that the blue finance field is rapidly evolving and requires continuous learning and adaptation.

A Call for Integration, Innovation, and Inclusion

At its core, blue finance is about more than financial engineering, it is about systems change. Success demands integration across sectors (environment, finance, infrastructure, fisheries), scales (local, national, regional, global), and stakeholders (public, private, philanthropic, community, Indigenous). It demands innovation, not just in instruments but in governance, measurement, and stakeholder engagement. And it demands a commitment to inclusion, recognizing the rights, knowledge, and agency of those who depend most directly on healthy oceans.

Readers of this book are invited to see themselves as part of a growing movement: one that seeks to reconcile economic ambition with planetary boundaries, climate risk with nature-based resilience, and profit with purpose. Whether you are a policymaker shaping the next generation of blue economy strategies, a finance professional structuring a blue bond, a community leader developing a coastal restoration project, or a researcher exploring ocean solutions, the aim is to equip you with actionable insights, frameworks, and pathways.

Looking Ahead

As we enter what many see as the "decade of ocean action," the stakes and the opportunities have never been greater. The decisions made in the coming years, about what we finance, how we invest, and who benefits, will shape not just the health of the oceans but the future of societies and economies worldwide. Blue finance provides both a vision and a toolbox for navigating this critical juncture.

The chapters that follow will delve deeper into the mechanics, governance, and future trends of blue finance, offering a roadmap for unlocking the potential of the world's greatest shared resource. The path ahead will require ambition, cooperation, and a willingness to rethink old paradigms. But by aligning finance with the needs of the ocean, we can lay the foundation for a sustainable, resilient, and inclusive blue economy, one that benefits both people and planet, now and for generations to come.

Chapter 1: Understanding the Blue Economy and the Finance Gap

The blue economy encompasses the diverse range of economic activities that depend on healthy oceans, seas, and coasts, from fisheries and tourism to shipping, renewable energy, and biotechnology. Despite its vast potential to drive sustainable growth and human wellbeing, the blue economy faces persistent threats from overexploitation, pollution, and inadequate governance. At the heart of these challenges is a chronic gap between the scale of investment required to maintain ocean health and the resources currently available. This chapter introduces the concept of the blue economy, unpacks its economic and ecological significance, and assesses the market failures and externalities that hinder sustainability. It quantifies the magnitude of the global investment gap and explores why traditional finance mechanisms have struggled to bridge it. By highlighting the central role that finance plays in the transition from exploitative to regenerative marine systems, the chapter establishes a foundation for understanding the urgent need for new, innovative, and targeted blue finance instruments, setting the stage for the solutions explored in subsequent chapters.

Definition and Scope of the Sustainable Ocean Economy

The concept of the blue economy has rapidly gained prominence as nations, financial institutions, and multilateral organizations recognize the urgent need to align economic growth with the sustainable use of ocean resources. The blue economy can be defined as the range of economic activities that are directly or indirectly linked to the oceans, seas, and coasts. This definition encompasses both established sectors, such as fisheries, shipping, and coastal tourism, and emerging industries, including offshore renewable energy, aquaculture, and marine biotechnology. Unlike the traditional marine economy, which often prioritized extraction and exploitation, the blue economy is explicitly grounded in principles of environmental stewardship, social equity, and long-term economic viability.

The scope of the sustainable ocean economy extends well beyond sectoral boundaries. It requires a holistic approach that recognizes the interconnectedness of natural systems, economic activities, and community well-being. This means moving away from isolated sectoral management towards integrated ocean governance frameworks that balance economic development with ecological health. The sustainable ocean economy also emphasizes the need to restore and protect the underlying natural capital, the ecosystems and biodiversity that support all ocean-based industries. Healthy marine ecosystems provide services such as carbon sequestration, climate regulation, coastal protection, and food security, all of which are critical for global sustainability.

Furthermore, the blue economy is inherently cross-cutting, interfacing with global priorities such as climate change mitigation and adaptation, poverty alleviation, gender equality, and the achievement of the United Nations Sustainable Development Goals (SDGs), particularly SDG 14, Life Below Water. As the impacts of climate change and unsustainable exploitation become increasingly evident, the sustainable ocean economy is positioned not only as a pathway for economic resilience and growth but as an imperative for planetary health and social stability. Realizing the full potential of the blue economy, however, demands targeted investments, coordinated policies, and robust financial mechanisms that channel resources towards regenerative and inclusive models of ocean use.

Economic Sectors in the Blue Economy (e.g., Fisheries, Transport, Tourism, Renewables)

The blue economy is composed of a diverse array of sectors, each playing a distinct role in the economic and social fabric of coastal and island nations. Traditional sectors remain central to livelihoods and food security, while newer industries offer pathways for innovation and sustainable growth.

Fisheries and Aquaculture: Fisheries have long been the backbone of the ocean economy, providing nutrition and employment for millions globally. Sustainable fisheries management is critical, given that overfishing and illegal, unreported, and unregulated (IUU) fishing threaten the health of marine ecosystems and the viability of fish stocks. Aquaculture, when practiced responsibly, offers an alternative that can reduce pressure on wild populations and enhance food security.

Marine Transport and Shipping: The maritime transport sector is vital to global trade, with over 80% of world merchandise trade by volume carried by sea. Modernizing fleets for energy efficiency, reducing emissions, and preventing marine pollution are pressing challenges for the industry as it seeks to align with climate goals.

Coastal and Marine Tourism: Tourism along coastlines and in marine areas is a significant source of revenue for many countries, especially small island developing states (SIDS). However, unmanaged tourism can drive habitat degradation, pollution, and resource depletion. Sustainable tourism initiatives are essential for balancing economic benefits with environmental protection.

Offshore Renewable Energy: Harnessing the power of wind, waves, and tides presents vast opportunities for clean energy generation. Offshore wind, in particular, has seen substantial growth, supported by falling costs and technological advances. These industries must be carefully sited and managed to minimize ecological impacts and ensure compatibility with other ocean uses.

Marine Biotechnology and Emerging Sectors: Advances in biotechnology are unlocking new products and services derived from marine organisms, from pharmaceuticals to biofuels. Deep-sea mining, while controversial due to its potential environmental risks, is also emerging as a sector with significant economic interests.

These sectors, both established and emergent, are interconnected and often compete for space and resources. Achieving a truly sustainable blue economy requires integrated ocean planning, investment in innovation, and strong governance to manage trade-offs and synergies across sectors. This will ensure that economic benefits are realized in harmony with social equity and ecosystem integrity.

Market Failures and Environmental Externalities in Ocean Resource Use

Despite the economic value generated by the ocean economy, pervasive market failures and externalities have led to widespread degradation of marine resources and ecosystems. The ocean's vastness, interconnectedness, and open-access nature make it especially vulnerable to unsustainable exploitation and insufficient stewardship.

Tragedy of the Commons: The classic "tragedy of the commons" is especially pronounced in the marine environment, where weak property rights and inadequate regulation allow individuals or entities to over-extract resources or pollute with minimal accountability. This results in overfishing, destruction of habitats such as coral reefs and mangroves, and the accumulation of marine pollution.

Environmental Externalities: Many ocean-based economic activities impose negative externalities, uncompensated costs, on society and the environment. For instance, commercial shipping can lead to oil spills, ballast water discharges, and air pollution, impacting coastal communities and marine biodiversity. Similarly, land-based sources of pollution, such as agricultural runoff and untreated sewage, contribute to dead zones and coral bleaching, with long-term ecological and economic consequences.

Lack of Valuation of Ecosystem Services: Traditional markets have failed to recognize and value the vital ecosystem services provided by healthy oceans, such as carbon sequestration, shoreline protection, and nutrient cycling. As a result, these services are undervalued or ignored in investment and policy decisions, leading to their depletion.

Short-Termism and Subsidies: Economic incentives often favor short-term profits over long-term sustainability. Harmful subsidies, particularly in fisheries and fossil fuels, distort markets by encouraging overexploitation and environmentally damaging practices. According to the OECD, global fisheries subsidies are estimated at over $35 billion per year, much of which supports overfishing.

Information Asymmetry and Governance Gaps: Information on the status of marine resources and the impacts of various activities is often incomplete, inconsistent, or inaccessible, leading to suboptimal decision-making. Additionally, fragmented governance at local, national, and international levels creates loopholes and weakens enforcement of regulations.

Inequitable Access and Benefit Sharing: Market failures are also social in nature. Marginalized groups, including small-scale fishers and coastal communities, often lack secure rights to marine resources or fair access to benefits. This can exacerbate poverty and undermine efforts to achieve inclusive and sustainable development.

Addressing these market failures requires a multi-pronged approach:

- Establishing clear property rights and marine spatial planning to allocate resources efficiently
- Internalizing externalities through regulation, pollution taxes, and removal of harmful subsidies
- Mainstreaming natural capital accounting and ecosystem service valuation in economic planning
- Enhancing transparency and access to information
- Strengthening governance structures to ensure accountability and inclusivity

By correcting these failures, blue finance can help realign economic incentives, drive investment into sustainable practices, and ensure that the true value of ocean ecosystems is recognized in financial flows.

Quantifying the Global Investment Gap for Ocean Sustainability

Securing a sustainable future for the world's oceans demands a fundamental transformation in how marine resources are financed and managed. Despite widespread recognition of the importance of healthy oceans, the scale of current investments falls dramatically short of what is needed to achieve global sustainability goals.

Defining the Investment Gap: The global investment gap in the blue economy refers to the difference between existing financial flows and the estimated resources required to restore, protect, and sustain marine and coastal ecosystems. Estimates of the blue finance gap vary, but all suggest a massive shortfall. According to the High Level Panel for a Sustainable Ocean Economy, at least $175 billion per year is required to achieve SDG 14 and ensure healthy ocean ecosystems, yet only a fraction of this amount is mobilized annually.

Drivers of the Investment Gap:

- **High Perceived Risk:** Many investors view ocean-related projects as high-risk due to regulatory uncertainty, insufficient data, and the complexity of marine ecosystems. This raises the cost of capital and deters private sector participation.
- **Limited Pipeline of Bankable Projects:** There is a lack of well-developed, investment-ready projects in the blue economy, particularly in developing countries. Project development and preparation are resource-intensive and require technical expertise, which may be lacking.
- **Underdeveloped Financial Instruments:** Traditional finance mechanisms are often ill-suited to the unique needs

15

of the ocean sector. For example, most insurance products and collateralization models do not adequately capture natural capital or ecosystem services, limiting access to finance.

- **Institutional Barriers:** Fragmented mandates, overlapping jurisdictions, and weak coordination among government agencies and donors hinder efficient allocation of resources.

Quantifying the Gap by Sector:

- **Marine Protected Areas (MPAs):** Global funding for MPAs covers only a small portion of the area needed to achieve conservation targets. A UNEP report found that less than 10% of the annual funding required for effective MPA management is currently available.
- **Sustainable Fisheries and Aquaculture:** Investments in sustainable fisheries management and responsible aquaculture are estimated to require tens of billions of dollars per year, with the actual flows falling well short of this need.
- **Ocean Renewable Energy:** The International Renewable Energy Agency (IRENA) notes that closing the gap in offshore wind and other marine renewables will require over $1 trillion in investment by 2050 to align with Paris Agreement targets.
- **Pollution Control and Coastal Resilience:** The cost of addressing marine pollution and building coastal resilience, such as restoring mangroves, coral reefs, and wetlands, runs into the hundreds of billions globally.

Consequences of the Investment Gap: Failure to close the investment gap undermines global efforts to combat climate change, halt biodiversity loss, and protect vulnerable communities from the impacts of sea level rise, ocean acidification, and extreme weather events. It also limits opportunities for sustainable economic growth, job creation, and poverty reduction.

Opportunities for Closing the Gap:

- **Leveraging Public Finance:** Public funds can play a catalytic role in reducing risk, building capacity, and crowding in private investment through blended finance models.
- **Innovative Financing Instruments:** Mechanisms such as blue bonds, debt-for-nature swaps, and impact investing vehicles can mobilize new sources of capital.
- **Strengthening Project Preparation:** Support for early-stage project development, technical assistance, and pipeline-building is critical.
- **Enhancing Data and Transparency:** Improved data collection, monitoring, and reporting can lower perceived risk and increase investor confidence.

A concerted, multi-stakeholder approach is needed to mobilize the scale of finance required to restore ocean health, build resilience, and deliver on global commitments. Blue finance, as a set of innovative tools and frameworks, is at the heart of these efforts.

The Role of Finance in Transitioning from Exploitative to Regenerative Marine Systems

Finance serves as both a lever and a barrier in shaping the future of the world's oceans. For decades, conventional finance models enabled and even encouraged the overexploitation of marine resources, prioritizing short-term returns over long-term sustainability. Reversing this trajectory requires a fundamental shift: directing capital away from extractive activities toward investments that restore, regenerate, and sustain ocean ecosystems and the communities that depend on them.

Enabling Regenerative Approaches: Regenerative marine systems go beyond minimizing harm, they seek to repair damage, enhance ecosystem functions, and create positive social outcomes. Examples include investments in restoring coastal habitats (such as mangroves and seagrasses), adopting sustainable fisheries practices, and supporting innovations that reduce plastic and nutrient pollution.

Finance is essential for scaling these solutions, as they often require significant upfront investment, cross-sector coordination, and patient capital with longer time horizons.

The Power of Blue Finance Instruments: The rise of blue finance has introduced a new set of tools, such as blue bonds, debt-for-nature swaps, and blended finance facilities, that are designed to redirect capital toward positive environmental and social outcomes. Blue bonds, for example, earmark proceeds for ocean conservation and sustainable economic activity, while debt-for-nature swaps reduce debt burdens for developing countries in exchange for commitments to marine protection. These instruments leverage public, private, and philanthropic capital to fill gaps left by traditional funding sources.

Aligning Incentives and Risk: Effective blue finance mechanisms align financial incentives with the long-term health of the ocean. This means embedding sustainability criteria, rigorous reporting, and adaptive management into financial products and investment decision-making. Innovative risk-sharing approaches, such as credit guarantees and insurance products, can help de-risk projects and attract a wider range of investors. Meanwhile, aligning finance with global frameworks, such as the SDGs, Paris Agreement, and Convention on Biological Diversity, ensures that investments support internationally agreed objectives.

Supporting Inclusive and Equitable Transitions: Transitioning to regenerative marine systems also demands attention to equity and inclusion. Finance can empower coastal and Indigenous communities by supporting locally led conservation, enabling access to credit and markets, and recognizing traditional knowledge and rights. This inclusive approach not only delivers better social outcomes but also improves the effectiveness and sustainability of conservation investments.

Overcoming Barriers: Despite its promise, the transition to regenerative marine finance faces challenges. Many ocean investments generate returns over long timeframes and involve complex, multi-stakeholder processes. Standardizing metrics for impact, ensuring transparency, and addressing governance gaps are ongoing priorities. Strong enabling environments, comprising sound policies, institutional capacity, and supportive legal frameworks, are crucial for attracting and sustaining investment.

Catalyzing Systemic Change: Ultimately, the role of finance is to catalyze systemic change: shifting business models, market dynamics, and consumer behavior toward a future where healthy oceans underpin resilient economies and societies. Blue finance is not a panacea, but it provides a powerful set of levers for mobilizing the scale of investment needed for ocean regeneration. Through innovative mechanisms, partnerships, and policy coherence, finance can drive the transition from exploitation to stewardship, placing the sustainable ocean economy at the heart of a global green and blue recovery.

Chapter 2: Principles and Objectives of Blue Finance

Blue finance is more than a funding stream; it is a framework for aligning financial flows with the protection, sustainable use, and resilience of ocean and coastal resources. This chapter sets out the guiding principles and core objectives that underpin credible blue finance initiatives. It explains how blue finance can generate conservation outcomes, support climate resilience, and foster sustainable livelihoods for coastal communities. Key themes include the importance of additionality, accountability, and transparency in blue finance, as well as alignment with Sustainable Development Goal 14 and broader climate targets. The chapter also explores how nature-positive outcomes and ESG (environmental, social, and governance) metrics are integrated into the design and management of blue finance. By clarifying what distinguishes blue finance from other forms of sustainable finance, this chapter provides the conceptual grounding needed to design, assess, and evaluate effective financial mechanisms that genuinely support the health of marine ecosystems and the prosperity of those who depend on them.

Definition and Characteristics of Blue Finance

Blue finance is an evolving field of sustainable finance that channels capital to projects, activities, and assets that contribute directly to the protection, restoration, and sustainable use of ocean and coastal ecosystems. It is distinguished from traditional finance by its explicit commitment to advancing environmental, social, and economic objectives specific to the marine context. At its core, blue finance mobilizes public, private, and blended capital through a range of instruments, such as blue bonds, grants, guarantees, and impact funds, to enable a sustainable ocean economy.

What sets blue finance apart is its sectoral and outcome-based orientation. Blue finance does not simply fund economic activity near or in the ocean; it seeks to ensure that investments result in measurable positive impacts for ocean health, climate resilience, and community well-being. To achieve this, blue finance instruments are underpinned by rigorous eligibility criteria, sustainability frameworks, and reporting requirements that align with international norms and standards, including the United Nations SDGs.

Key characteristics of blue finance include:

- **Purpose-driven Capital Allocation:** Funds are earmarked for marine conservation, pollution reduction, sustainable fisheries, clean shipping, renewable marine energy, and related activities.
- **Impact Orientation:** Investment decisions are informed by science-based metrics and monitoring systems that track environmental and social outcomes.
- **Risk Management:** Blue finance mechanisms integrate risk assessment specific to ocean-based activities, including climate risks, regulatory uncertainty, and market volatility.
- **Partnership and Collaboration:** Success in blue finance often depends on multi-stakeholder partnerships involving governments, development finance institutions, NGOs, and local communities.
- **Innovation and Flexibility:** Given the dynamic nature of marine systems and blue economy sectors, blue finance continually adapts through the development of new financial instruments and models, such as blended finance, payment for ecosystem services, and tokenized impact assets.

As global attention turns to the ocean as both a source of opportunity and a front line of environmental crisis, blue finance provides a critical vehicle for scaling up investment, driving systemic change, and ensuring that the benefits of the blue economy are realized equitably and sustainably.

Key Objectives: Conservation, Sustainable Use, Resilience, Livelihoods

The primary objectives of blue finance are closely linked to the triple bottom line, people, planet, and prosperity, with a particular emphasis on delivering tangible improvements in ocean health and coastal community resilience. Each objective is mutually reinforcing, supporting the long-term viability of the blue economy.

1. Conservation:

At the heart of blue finance is the imperative to halt and reverse marine ecosystem degradation. This includes financing the protection of biodiversity, the establishment and effective management of MPAs, the restoration of critical habitats such as coral reefs and mangroves, and the reduction of threats from pollution and overexploitation. Conservation finance, as a subset of blue finance, aims to safeguard natural capital that underpins food security, climate regulation, and economic productivity.

2. Sustainable Use:

Blue finance supports the transition from extractive and polluting practices toward sustainable use of marine resources. This means financing the adoption of best practices in fisheries management, supporting eco-certified aquaculture, promoting circular economy models to reduce waste, and incentivizing low-impact shipping and marine tourism. Sustainable use is not about halting economic activity in the ocean but about ensuring that development remains within ecological limits and generates net-positive outcomes.

3. Resilience:

Climate change and rising ocean risks, such as sea-level rise, extreme weather events, and ocean acidification, underscore the need for resilience-building investments. Blue finance aims to enhance the adaptive capacity of both natural systems and human communities. This is achieved by funding infrastructure and nature-based solutions (e.g., living shorelines, coastal wetlands), supporting risk assessment and early warning systems, and facilitating the development of insurance and risk-sharing products for climate-vulnerable sectors.

4. Livelihoods and Social Inclusion:

A central objective of blue finance is to improve the livelihoods of those who depend most directly on ocean resources, including small-scale fishers, Indigenous peoples, and coastal communities. This requires supporting inclusive business models, ensuring fair benefit sharing, and providing access to capital, technical assistance, and markets. Empowering communities through participatory finance mechanisms and community-led conservation increases both the effectiveness and the social legitimacy of blue finance initiatives.

By integrating these objectives into financial flows, blue finance offers a pathway to achieving the SDGs, with SDG 14 (Life Below Water) at its center but also with positive impacts on poverty reduction, gender equality, and climate action.

Core Principles: Additionality, Accountability, Transparency, Alignment with SDG 14 and Climate Goals

Robust principles underpin blue finance to ensure it delivers real, measurable, and lasting change for ocean ecosystems and societies. The most widely recognized principles are:

Additionality:

Blue finance must generate benefits that would not have occurred in the absence of the intervention or investment. This "additionality" is critical for preventing the relabeling of business-as-usual activities as sustainable or "blue." For example, a blue bond must finance new or expanded conservation efforts, not simply fund existing operations. Demonstrating additionality builds trust among investors, regulators, and beneficiaries, and is a precondition for accessing many public and philanthropic funding streams.

Accountability:

Financial flows in blue finance must be tracked and reported in a manner that ensures investments are used as intended and that results are delivered. Accountability is achieved through:

- Clearly defined use-of-proceeds frameworks in bonds and loans
- Binding commitments and performance targets in funding agreements
- Regular monitoring, evaluation, and third-party verification

Effective accountability systems deter misuse of funds and support adaptive management, allowing course corrections when projects fall short of targets or encounter unforeseen challenges.

Transparency:

Transparency is foundational for attracting capital, managing risk, and maintaining the integrity of blue finance. Investors and stakeholders require access to accurate, timely information about project selection, financial flows, environmental and social performance, and the governance of blue finance vehicles. High transparency standards reduce information asymmetries, lower transaction costs, and build a stronger investment case. Examples include publicly disclosed impact reports, open-access data portals, and stakeholder engagement in project design and monitoring.

Alignment with SDG 14 and Climate Goals:

Blue finance instruments must be closely aligned with global frameworks and goals, notably SDG 14 ("Conserve and sustainably use the oceans, seas and marine resources for sustainable development") and the Paris Agreement on climate change. This alignment ensures that financial flows support international commitments and that investments have a coherent, cumulative effect at the global level.

- For SDG 14, alignment means prioritizing projects that directly contribute to targets such as ending overfishing, reducing marine pollution, protecting coastal ecosystems, and increasing ocean-based scientific knowledge.
- For climate goals, blue finance supports both mitigation (e.g., through carbon sequestration in marine ecosystems or renewable energy) and adaptation (e.g., through risk reduction and coastal resilience investments).

Other Relevant Principles:

- **Stakeholder Inclusion:** Blue finance should be participatory, with meaningful involvement of affected communities and stakeholders in design, decision-making, and benefit sharing.
- **Do No Harm:** Projects must avoid unintended negative consequences for people or the environment, with rigorous safeguards in place.
- **Adaptive Management:** Blue finance recognizes the complexity and dynamism of ocean systems, embedding flexibility and learning into finance structures.

Collectively, these principles safeguard the credibility of blue finance, ensure it delivers on its promise, and make it possible for public, private, and blended capital to flow at scale into ocean-positive outcomes.

Integration of Nature-Positive and Climate-Resilient Outcomes in Financing

Blue finance is at its most transformative when it intentionally integrates nature-positive and climate-resilient outcomes into the design, structuring, and management of financial instruments and investments. These dual outcomes are mutually reinforcing: healthy, functioning ecosystems are more resilient to climate impacts, while climate adaptation and mitigation efforts that protect or restore nature deliver broader social and economic benefits.

Nature-Positive Finance:

A nature-positive approach ensures that investments result in net gains for biodiversity and ecosystem health. This moves beyond minimizing environmental damage ("do no harm") to proactively restoring degraded habitats, rewilding coastal zones, and re-establishing ecosystem services. Nature-positive finance is embedded in projects that, for example:

- Fund the replanting of mangroves for carbon sequestration and coastal protection
- Restore coral reefs to increase biodiversity and boost tourism revenues
- Rehabilitate seagrass meadows to support fisheries and absorb carbon

These interventions are supported by robust impact metrics and monitored for both ecological and socio-economic outcomes.

Climate-Resilient Finance:

Investing for climate resilience means directing finance toward activities that reduce vulnerability to climate change, increase adaptive capacity, and support disaster risk reduction. This is especially critical for SIDS, least developed countries, and vulnerable coastal communities. Climate-resilient blue finance might include:

- Supporting early warning systems for ocean-based hazards

- Building or restoring "green-grey" infrastructure (e.g., combining seawalls with living shorelines)
- Financing insurance products for small-scale fishers

Operationalizing Integration:

The integration of nature-positive and climate-resilient outcomes is operationalized through:

- Cross-sector collaboration (e.g., combining conservation finance with infrastructure or livelihood projects)
- Setting dual-impact objectives and performance indicators
- Leveraging blended finance to align different investor priorities and risk appetites

By mainstreaming these outcomes in all blue finance flows, financial markets and institutions help ensure that ocean investments do not simply maintain the status quo, but actively drive the transition to a regenerative, climate-proof blue economy.

Links Between Blue Finance and Environmental, Social, and Governance Metrics

ESG metrics are now a cornerstone of responsible investment across all sectors. Blue finance leverages ESG frameworks both as a tool for aligning investments with sustainability objectives and as a means to unlock larger pools of capital from mainstream investors seeking to manage risk and demonstrate impact.

Environmental Metrics:

In the blue finance context, environmental metrics extend beyond carbon emissions to include indicators such as:

- Marine biodiversity (species richness, habitat area)

- Ecosystem health (water quality, presence of keystone species)
- Pollution reduction (e.g., plastics, nutrient runoff)
- Resource efficiency (sustainable fisheries, aquaculture certification)

These metrics allow investors to assess the ecological value-add of their investments and to monitor compliance with regulatory or voluntary standards.

Social Metrics:

Social dimensions are especially important in the ocean context, given the close dependence of millions on marine resources. Key social metrics include:

- Job creation in sustainable blue economy sectors
- Livelihood security for small-scale fishers and coastal populations
- Gender equality and women's participation
- Community engagement and empowerment
- Access to education and capacity building

Blue finance structures often include requirements for social impact assessments, local hiring and procurement, and ongoing stakeholder consultation.

Governance Metrics:

Strong governance underpins effective blue finance. ESG governance criteria in blue finance cover:

- Transparency and disclosure practices
- Anti-corruption and anti-money laundering measures
- Board and management diversity
- Stakeholder participation in decision-making

- Adherence to international legal and regulatory frameworks

Effective governance reduces reputational and regulatory risks, improves project outcomes, and supports investor confidence.

Integrating ESG into Blue Finance Products:

Many blue finance instruments, such as blue bonds and loans, are now designed with ESG requirements embedded into covenants, reporting structures, and performance indicators. For example, issuers of blue bonds may be required to provide regular, third-party verified reports on ESG outcomes, as well as to comply with global best practice frameworks like the ICMA Green and Blue Bond Principles.

Unlocking Capital Through ESG:

Mainstreaming ESG in blue finance increases the attractiveness of ocean investments to institutional investors, pension funds, and asset managers who are increasingly bound by ESG mandates. This is particularly relevant as regulatory frameworks evolve to require disclosure of environmental and social risks, such as the EU Sustainable Finance Disclosure Regulation (SFDR) and the Task Force on Nature-related Financial Disclosures (TNFD).

By embedding ESG throughout the investment process, blue finance can unlock capital at scale, improve risk-adjusted returns, and ensure that financial flows deliver positive outcomes for people and planet.

Chapter 3: Blue Bonds as a Mechanism for Ocean Investment

Blue bonds have rapidly emerged as one of the most visible and promising tools for mobilizing investment in the sustainable ocean economy. These specialized debt instruments channel capital directly to marine and coastal projects that deliver measurable environmental and social impact. This chapter examines the core structure and function of blue bonds, highlighting how they differ from traditional green and sustainability bonds. It unpacks the critical design elements, such as use of proceeds, reporting frameworks, and impact metrics, that ensure transparency, integrity, and credibility. The chapter also discusses the diversity of blue bond issuers, from sovereign governments to corporations and multilateral institutions, and identifies key challenges in scaling the blue bond market globally. By demystifying the mechanics of blue bonds and providing actionable insights for issuers and investors, this chapter positions blue bonds as a cornerstone of the broader blue finance landscape.

Structure and Function of Blue Bonds

Blue bonds are an innovative financing tool specifically designed to mobilize capital for the protection, restoration, and sustainable use of ocean and coastal resources. At their core, blue bonds are debt securities issued to investors, with the explicit commitment that proceeds will be used exclusively for projects and activities generating positive environmental, social, and economic outcomes in the marine and coastal context. The advent of blue bonds responds to the global investment gap in ocean sustainability, providing governments, development agencies, and private sector actors with a dedicated mechanism to fund the blue economy.

The structure of a blue bond closely mirrors that of conventional fixed-income instruments: an issuer, such as a sovereign government, development bank, or corporation, raises funds from investors in exchange for regular interest payments and the repayment of principal at maturity. What distinguishes blue bonds is the binding use-of-proceeds requirement: all capital raised must be earmarked for ocean-positive purposes. Eligible activities commonly include establishing and managing marine protected areas, restoring coral reefs, supporting sustainable fisheries and aquaculture, reducing marine pollution, and developing climate-resilient coastal infrastructure.

The issuance process involves several key stages:

- **Project Identification:** The issuer identifies a portfolio of eligible projects that meet pre-defined environmental and social criteria.
- **Bond Structuring:** Terms are set, including maturity, coupon rate, currency, and risk mitigation features such as guarantees or credit enhancements if required.
- **Certification and Reporting:** Independent, third-party review is typically conducted to verify the alignment of projects with recognized blue finance standards and to provide assurance to investors regarding the integrity of the bond.
- **Monitoring and Evaluation:** Proceeds are managed in a ring-fenced manner, and issuers commit to ongoing impact monitoring, annual reporting, and evaluation against pre-agreed metrics.

The function of blue bonds is threefold:

- **Capital Mobilization:** By offering a liquid, standardized product, blue bonds appeal to a broad investor base, including institutional investors, pension funds, and asset managers seeking to align portfolios with ESG and impact goals.
- **Signaling Effect:** Blue bonds send a powerful market signal about the importance and investability of ocean conservation and sustainable blue economy activities, helping to

31

mainstream blue finance within the wider sustainable finance ecosystem.

- **Capacity Building:** The process of developing, issuing, and reporting on blue bonds strengthens issuer capabilities in environmental risk management, project pipeline development, and stakeholder engagement.

Notably, the blue bond concept was first piloted in 2018 by the Republic of Seychelles, which issued a $15 million sovereign blue bond to support sustainable marine and fisheries projects. Since then, the model has expanded, with multilateral development banks, corporates, and other sovereigns exploring or launching blue bond programs tailored to their specific needs and contexts.

Blue bonds, when rigorously structured and governed, represent a powerful lever for scaling investment in marine and coastal sustainability, linking global capital markets to the achievement of ocean and climate objectives.

Differences from Green and Sustainability Bonds

While blue bonds are built upon the foundation established by green and sustainability bonds, they possess distinctive features and serve unique purposes within the landscape of sustainable finance. Understanding these differences is crucial for issuers, investors, and policymakers seeking to utilize these instruments effectively.

Thematic Focus:

Green bonds are debt securities whose proceeds finance projects with explicit environmental benefits, most commonly in areas such as renewable energy, energy efficiency, pollution prevention, and sustainable agriculture. Sustainability bonds, meanwhile, target projects with both environmental and social impacts, often bridging climate action with outcomes like poverty reduction or health improvement. Blue bonds, however, are exclusively dedicated to projects that deliver measurable benefits to marine and coastal ecosystems, as well as the communities dependent on them.

Eligibility Criteria:

Blue bonds require project eligibility frameworks tailored to the unique characteristics of the ocean economy. This includes criteria for sustainable fisheries management, marine protected areas, coastal infrastructure, pollution control, and biodiversity restoration, areas often overlooked by broader green bond standards. Blue bond frameworks frequently incorporate marine-specific science, standards, and stakeholder consultation processes to ensure alignment with global best practice.

Impact Measurement:

The metrics and impact assessment protocols for blue bonds differ from those of green and sustainability bonds due to the distinctive challenges of monitoring ocean health, biodiversity, and the resilience of coastal communities. Blue bonds often require specialized indicators, such as changes in fish stocks, extent of habitat restored, or reductions in plastic pollution, rather than more general measures of emissions reduction or energy savings.

Stakeholder Involvement and Co-Benefits:

Given the shared nature of marine resources and the critical importance of inclusive governance in the ocean context, blue bond design frequently places a higher emphasis on participatory approaches, Indigenous and local community engagement, and benefit-sharing arrangements.

Market Development:

The blue bond market remains nascent compared to the green bond market, which exceeded $500 billion in annual issuance in 2023. As such, blue bond issuances often require additional capacity building, technical assistance, and partnership with multilateral development institutions to develop pipelines and ensure market integrity.

In summary, while blue, green, and sustainability bonds are all valuable tools for channeling capital to positive environmental and social outcomes, blue bonds fill a distinct gap by directly targeting the finance needs of ocean ecosystems and blue economy sectors. Their specialized nature is both a strength and a challenge, requiring bespoke frameworks and innovative approaches to scale.

Issuer Types (Sovereign, Municipal, Corporate, Multilateral)

A variety of entities are eligible to issue blue bonds, each bringing different advantages, risk profiles, and market reach. Understanding the spectrum of issuer types is vital for designing blue bond programs that are well-aligned with policy, operational, and investment objectives.

Sovereign Issuers:

National governments, especially those of coastal and island nations, are key players in the blue bond market. Sovereign blue bonds enable countries to access international capital markets for the explicit purpose of advancing marine conservation, climate adaptation, and sustainable development goals. These bonds often support national ocean strategies, fisheries management reforms, or the expansion of marine protected areas. Sovereign blue bonds can attract concessional finance and guarantees from multilateral institutions to enhance creditworthiness, as demonstrated by the pioneering Seychelles Blue Bond.

Municipal and Sub-National Issuers:

Sub-national governments, such as states, provinces, or municipalities, may issue blue bonds to finance local coastal resilience projects, sustainable infrastructure, or urban marine ecosystem restoration. Municipal blue bonds are well suited to contexts where urbanization is putting pressure on coastal environments and where city governments have clear mandates for infrastructure investment and environmental management.

Corporate Issuers:

Corporations with operations linked to the ocean economy, such as shipping lines, seafood companies, tourism operators, or renewable energy developers, are increasingly able to issue blue bonds to finance sustainability initiatives. These bonds may fund efforts to decarbonize fleets, implement sustainable supply chains, or restore marine habitats affected by business activities. Corporate blue bonds can improve a company's ESG profile, attract impact-oriented investors, and differentiate products or services in increasingly conscious markets.

Multilateral Development Banks and International Financial Institutions (IFIs):

MDBs and IFIs, such as the World Bank, Asian Development Bank, and African Development Bank, play a pivotal role as both issuers and supporters of blue bonds. They may issue blue bonds themselves to finance a portfolio of regional or global ocean projects, or they may provide technical assistance, credit enhancements, and co-financing to enable sovereign or municipal issuances. MDB-backed blue bonds can accelerate market development, build local capacity, and reduce perceived risk for investors.

The diversity of issuer types expands the reach and potential impact of blue bonds, allowing the instrument to be tailored to the specific investment needs, governance contexts, and market access of a wide range of stakeholders. Careful alignment of issuer strategy with national and global ocean finance priorities maximizes both impact and market credibility.

Key Design Elements: Use of Proceeds, Reporting Frameworks, Impact Metrics

The credibility and effectiveness of blue bonds hinge on robust design elements that guarantee transparency, integrity, and measurable outcomes. Investors and stakeholders demand clarity and accountability regarding how capital is deployed and what impact is achieved. Key design elements include:

1. Use of Proceeds:

All blue bond frameworks require that proceeds be earmarked exclusively for eligible projects that deliver tangible ocean-positive outcomes. The use-of-proceeds section of a blue bond prospectus is highly detailed, typically referencing a recognized taxonomy or criteria for project selection. Eligible uses might include:

- Marine protected area establishment or management
- Sustainable fisheries and aquaculture projects
- Pollution reduction (e.g., waste management, water treatment)
- Coastal resilience infrastructure
- Nature-based solutions for shoreline protection
- Marine renewable energy installations

Issuers must demonstrate that funds are "ring-fenced", segregated from general revenue and traceable throughout the project lifecycle. This ensures that blue bond proceeds are not inadvertently diverted to non-qualifying activities.

2. Project Evaluation and Selection:

A rigorous evaluation and selection process underpins project eligibility. This may involve internal screening by the issuer, third-party validation, and the establishment of an independent blue finance committee or advisory group. Criteria commonly assessed include:

- Alignment with blue finance principles and SDG 14 targets
- Environmental and social risk assessment
- Additionality (demonstrating the project is above and beyond business as usual)
- Stakeholder and community engagement processes

3. Reporting Frameworks:

Transparency and investor confidence are supported by comprehensive reporting frameworks. Issuers typically commit to:

- Annual reporting on allocation of proceeds, progress, and results
- Disclosure of any changes in project portfolio or management
- Third-party verification of reporting and impact data

Reports are made publicly available, with increasing emphasis on digital platforms that allow real-time tracking of investments and outcomes.

4. Impact Metrics:

Measuring and communicating impact is essential for both accountability and learning. Blue bond impact metrics are often bespoke, reflecting the complexity of ocean systems and the diversity of eligible activities. Common metrics include:

- Area (km²) of marine or coastal habitat protected or restored
- Number and status of fish stocks managed sustainably

- Reductions in pollutants entering the marine environment (plastic, nutrients, etc.)
- Number of jobs or livelihoods created in blue economy sectors
- Carbon sequestration or emissions avoided through nature-based solutions

Issuers may draw on internationally recognized standards, such as those developed by the International Capital Market Association (ICMA), the Blue Natural Capital Financing Facility, or regional taxonomies tailored to local contexts.

5. Governance and Oversight:

Robust governance structures are built into blue bond design, typically involving:

- Establishment of an independent steering or oversight committee
- Regular stakeholder engagement, particularly with affected communities, NGOs, and Indigenous groups
- Mechanisms for grievance redress and adaptive management

6. Risk Management and Safeguards:

Given the inherent risks of marine projects (e.g., regulatory changes, climate impacts, ecosystem uncertainties), issuers embed risk mitigation strategies into bond design. These may include insurance products, guarantees, or contingency funds.

The convergence of these design elements ensures that blue bonds meet the highest standards of sustainability, integrity, and impact. Well-structured blue bonds inspire investor confidence, enable scaling, and drive tangible change for ocean health and resilience.

Challenges in Scaling the Blue Bond Market

Despite the clear potential of blue bonds, the market faces several structural and operational challenges that must be addressed to unlock capital at the scale required to transform the blue economy. Understanding these obstacles is critical for policymakers, issuers, and investors seeking to catalyze the next phase of growth.

1. Pipeline Development and Project Preparation:

A major constraint is the limited pipeline of "bankable" blue projects, those that are well-prepared, investment-ready, and capable of delivering clear financial returns and measurable environmental outcomes. Many developing countries, small island states, and local authorities lack the technical and financial resources needed to develop robust project proposals, conduct feasibility assessments, and structure deals that meet investor requirements. Dedicated project preparation facilities and technical assistance programs are essential for pipeline development.

2. Data Gaps and Impact Measurement:

Accurately monitoring and reporting the environmental and social impact of blue bond investments remains a challenge. Marine ecosystems are complex, data collection can be costly and logistically difficult, and standardized metrics are still evolving. Without credible, verifiable data, it is difficult to demonstrate additionality and maintain investor confidence. Continued investment in ocean science, technology, and monitoring systems is necessary.

3. Regulatory and Policy Uncertainty:

In many jurisdictions, regulatory frameworks governing the issuance and management of blue bonds are underdeveloped or absent. This creates uncertainty for issuers and investors alike. Moreover, policy instability, such as changes in marine spatial planning, resource rights, or environmental standards, can introduce additional risk and discourage long-term investment. Strengthening regulatory environments, developing blue finance taxonomies, and aligning policies with international norms are critical enablers.

4. Creditworthiness and Risk Perception:

Investors may perceive blue bond issuers, particularly in developing countries, as carrying higher credit risk, resulting in elevated borrowing costs or lack of access to capital markets. Credit enhancements, partial guarantees from MDBs, and blended finance mechanisms can help to mitigate risk and attract investors.

5. Market Awareness and Capacity:

The blue bond market is still in its infancy. Limited awareness among both issuers and investors, as well as a lack of capacity to develop, structure, and manage blue bonds, inhibits market growth. Scaling requires ongoing outreach, capacity building, knowledge exchange, and the creation of best practice platforms to share lessons and innovation.

6. Avoiding "Blue-washing":

A significant reputational risk is the possibility of "blue-washing," where issuers or investors claim blue credentials without delivering real or additional impact. Rigorous standards, third-party verification, and transparency are essential to guard against this risk and maintain market integrity.

7. Inclusivity and Equity:

Ensuring that blue bonds deliver benefits for marginalized groups, especially small-scale fishers, Indigenous peoples, and women, is a persistent challenge. Participatory design, equitable benefit-sharing mechanisms, and targeted support are needed to embed social justice in blue bond structures.

Addressing these challenges requires coordinated action by governments, development agencies, financial institutions, and civil society. If successful, blue bonds can become a cornerstone of ocean finance, channeling capital to the front lines of marine conservation, climate resilience, and sustainable blue growth.

Chapter 4: Debt-for-Nature Swaps and Sovereign Blue Finance

Debt-for-nature swaps offer a powerful means of reconciling fiscal sustainability with marine conservation, especially for coastal and island nations facing high debt burdens and urgent environmental threats. This chapter explores the evolution and application of debt-for-nature swaps, showing how they can be harnessed to convert external debt obligations into dedicated investments in marine and coastal resilience. It details the financial engineering and legal prerequisites needed for effective swaps, discusses the critical role of bilateral and multilateral creditors, and highlights the importance of aligning debt relief with national policy and long-term fiscal sustainability. By unpacking the mechanics and governance requirements of these instruments, the chapter demonstrates how sovereign blue finance strategies can unlock capital, drive systemic change, and enable countries to achieve their ocean and climate objectives, while also supporting broader economic and social development.

Overview of Debt-for-Nature Swaps and Their Application in Coastal States

Debt-for-nature swaps have emerged as a practical mechanism for aligning sovereign debt management with environmental conservation, particularly in countries where high debt burdens constrain public investment in sustainability. At their core, these transactions involve the restructuring or reduction of a country's external debt in exchange for commitments to fund nature-based or environmental protection activities. This instrument is especially pertinent to coastal and island states, which often grapple with mounting debt alongside pressing marine and climate challenges.

The basic logic of a debt-for-nature swap is straightforward but powerful. External creditors, whether bilateral governments, commercial banks, or multilateral institutions, agree to forgive, restructure, or sell a portion of a country's outstanding debt, often at a discount or on more favorable terms. In return, the debtor country agrees to use the equivalent value (or a negotiated share) of the debt relief for specific conservation investments, such as MPAs, habitat restoration, pollution control, sustainable fisheries management, or climate adaptation measures.

Debt-for-nature swaps were first popularized in the late 1980s and 1990s, typically focusing on terrestrial conservation in tropical countries. In the past decade, however, there has been growing recognition of their potential for blue finance, directing the proceeds of debt relief toward the sustainable management and protection of marine and coastal ecosystems. This is particularly relevant for SIDS and coastal countries, where economies are highly dependent on ocean resources, but fiscal space is constrained by debt service obligations.

Application in coastal states is particularly impactful due to:

- High levels of biodiversity and unique marine resources needing protection
- Vulnerability to climate change and disasters, which are exacerbated by debt overhangs
- Opportunities to link national development priorities with global environmental objectives, such as SDG 14 and the Paris Agreement

Successful blue debt swaps require not only innovative financial engineering but also robust legal frameworks, inclusive stakeholder engagement, and transparent governance to ensure that debt relief translates into real, measurable improvements in ocean and coastal resilience. They are increasingly being pursued as part of broader sovereign blue finance strategies, where fiscal stability, climate adaptation, and marine conservation are mutually reinforcing policy objectives.

Debt Conversion Structures and Financial Engineering for Conservation

The effectiveness of debt-for-nature swaps hinges on the specific financial structures and engineering solutions deployed. While each deal is unique, certain models and mechanisms have proven successful in maximizing both conservation impact and fiscal benefits for debtor nations.

1. Basic Model:

In its simplest form, a creditor agrees to cancel, reduce, or exchange a portion of sovereign debt. In return, the debtor government commits to direct local currency payments, usually over several years, into a conservation fund or directly to designated projects. This structure converts external debt obligations, often denominated in hard currency, into domestic investments that support marine or coastal priorities.

2. Buybacks and Debt Exchanges:

Sometimes, non-governmental organizations (NGOs) or international environmental funds act as intermediaries, purchasing debt from commercial banks or secondary markets at a discount. The NGO then negotiates with the debtor country to exchange the purchased debt for a commitment to local conservation spending. This allows for the leveraging of private capital and creates a multi-stakeholder governance structure around the funds.

3. Debt Swaps with Multilateral Support:

Multilateral development banks or international climate/environmental funds can facilitate more complex structures, such as blended finance or co-financing. For instance, the involvement of the World Bank or the Global Environment Facility (GEF) may provide technical assistance, guarantees, or concessional finance to reduce risk and enhance creditworthiness. These structures may include escrow accounts, independent fund trustees, and robust monitoring arrangements.

4. Blue Bonds Coupled with Debt Swaps:

A recent innovation involves issuing blue bonds as part of a debt conversion package. Here, debt relief is contingent upon the successful placement of blue bonds whose proceeds are earmarked for marine conservation. This approach leverages the growing appetite among investors for ESG and impact-linked bonds and creates a sustainable pipeline for future blue finance investments.

Key Financial Engineering Considerations:

- Setting appropriate discount rates and negotiating fair terms for all parties
- Ensuring sufficient scale to deliver meaningful conservation outcomes
- Designing payment schedules that align with fiscal realities and cash flows
- Creating safeguards to ensure conservation spending is additional, not substitutive

Debt-for-nature swaps offer a win-win proposition: creditors reduce exposure to distressed assets and demonstrate ESG leadership, while debtor nations gain fiscal space and direct capital to critical environmental priorities. Effective financial structuring is central to maximizing these benefits and ensuring the long-term success of the instrument.

Legal and Institutional Prerequisites for Implementation

Robust legal and institutional frameworks are foundational to the success and credibility of debt-for-nature swaps, particularly as they grow in complexity and ambition within blue finance. These prerequisites serve to safeguard the interests of all parties, ensure transparency, and deliver on conservation outcomes.

1. National Legal Frameworks:

The debtor country must have legal authority to enter into debt restructuring arrangements and to allocate public funds for environmental purposes. This often requires parliamentary approval, new regulations, or amendments to budget laws. Countries may need to establish or designate conservation trust funds, marine funds, or similar financial vehicles with clear mandates, governance structures, and fiduciary standards.

2. Creditor Consent and Legal Agreements:

For official bilateral debt, agreements must comply with international finance law and sometimes require coordination among multiple creditor governments. For commercial or multilateral debt, contractual terms must allow for assignment or sale to third parties (such as NGOs), and swap agreements must be carefully structured to avoid conflicts with bondholder rights, sovereign immunity, or cross-default clauses.

3. Environmental and Social Safeguards:

Legal documents must include binding commitments for the allocation of funds, the scope of eligible projects, and adherence to social and environmental safeguards. Independent oversight bodies or advisory committees, often with representation from government, civil society, and affected communities, are commonly established to ensure accountability and compliance.

4. Financial Management and Oversight:

Institutional arrangements must guarantee that conservation funds are professionally managed, ring-fenced from general government accounts, and protected from political interference. This may require the establishment of escrow accounts, appointment of independent trustees, and adoption of international best practices in financial management, auditing, and reporting.

5. Monitoring, Evaluation, and Transparency:

Legal frameworks should mandate regular monitoring and independent evaluation of project implementation and conservation impact. Results should be made publicly available, with clear grievance and feedback mechanisms for stakeholders.

6. Stakeholder Engagement:

The most effective debt-for-nature swaps are those that embed participatory processes throughout the lifecycle of the agreement, from negotiation to implementation to evaluation. This ensures buy-in from affected communities, reduces risks of social conflict, and enhances the legitimacy of conservation interventions.

7. International Legal Considerations:

Swaps must comply with global conventions and obligations, including the Paris Club principles, international anti-corruption standards, and treaties related to biodiversity and climate.

By fulfilling these legal and institutional prerequisites, debt-for-nature swaps can achieve durability, impact, and replicability, key features for scaling sovereign blue finance globally.

Role of Bilateral and Multilateral Creditors

Bilateral and multilateral creditors play pivotal roles in enabling, structuring, and scaling debt-for-nature swaps in the context of sovereign blue finance. Their actions and incentives determine both the feasibility and effectiveness of these instruments.

1. Bilateral Creditors:

Bilateral creditors, typically national governments, are often the largest holders of sovereign debt for many coastal and island states. They can initiate and negotiate swaps as part of broader development cooperation or foreign policy agendas. Debt-for-nature swaps offer these governments an opportunity to:

- Reduce non-performing or distressed assets on their balance sheets
- Demonstrate international leadership in climate and biodiversity finance
- Support the achievement of global commitments, such as the Convention on Biological Diversity (CBD) and the Paris Agreement

Bilateral creditors may agree to write down, reschedule, or convert a portion of debt in exchange for conservation spending. In many cases, they also provide technical assistance, capacity building, or co-financing for conservation activities.

2. Multilateral Creditors:

Multilateral development banks (MDBs) and international financial institutions (IFIs), such as the World Bank, African Development Bank, and IMF, can facilitate debt swaps in several ways:

- **Catalyzing Finance:** By providing concessional loans, guarantees, or blending facilities that reduce credit risk and enhance deal viability.
- **Convening and Mediation:** MDBs often serve as neutral intermediaries, bringing together debtor governments,

creditors, NGOs, and other stakeholders to design and
structure swaps.

- **Technical Assistance:** Support for policy reform, legal due
  diligence, project identification, and monitoring systems
  ensures that swaps deliver on environmental and fiscal
  objectives.
- **Capacity Building:** Training government officials and local
  partners to manage funds, implement projects, and report
  results builds the institutional strength needed for long-term
  success.

3. Private Creditors and NGOs:

While most debt-for-nature swaps involve official bilateral or
multilateral debt, there is a growing role for commercial creditors
and international NGOs. NGOs may purchase debt in secondary
markets or co-finance swaps, bringing expertise in conservation and
community engagement.

4. Multi-Creditor Coordination:

Many debtor countries have complex creditor profiles. Effective
swaps often require coordination among multiple creditor types,
official, multilateral, and private, to maximize scale, avoid
duplication, and align objectives.

5. Incentives and Barriers:

Creditors' willingness to participate is shaped by a mix of financial,
political, and reputational incentives, as well as by policy guidance
from international platforms such as the G20, Paris Club, and
UNFCCC. Barriers include administrative complexity, concerns
about moral hazard, and the need to balance financial integrity with
development goals.

6. Monitoring and Enforcement:

Both bilateral and multilateral creditors increasingly require robust monitoring and verification arrangements to ensure that debt relief is used as agreed. Third-party audits, independent evaluations, and transparent reporting build trust and facilitate replication.

The active and strategic engagement of creditors is essential for scaling up debt-for-nature swaps as a core tool in the sovereign blue finance toolkit.

Policy Alignment and Long-Term Fiscal Sustainability Considerations

For debt-for-nature swaps to deliver durable, system-wide benefits, they must be tightly aligned with national policies and integrated into long-term fiscal sustainability strategies. This ensures that short-term debt relief catalyzes lasting change in both conservation and development trajectories.

1. National Development Strategies:

Debt-for-nature swaps should be nested within broader national development and ocean economy plans, rather than being standalone interventions. Alignment with strategies for climate adaptation, biodiversity, blue economy, and disaster risk reduction maximizes synergy, avoids duplication, and embeds conservation into the fabric of national policy.

2. Fiscal Planning and Debt Management:

Swaps must be consistent with a country's medium- and long-term fiscal frameworks. This includes ensuring that debt relief does not inadvertently increase fiscal risk, undermine credit ratings, or crowd out other priority investments. Ministry of Finance engagement is crucial to structuring swaps that are fiscally neutral or positive over time.

3. Enabling Policy Environment:

To maximize impact, swaps should be accompanied by policy reforms that address underlying drivers of environmental degradation, such as weak governance, harmful subsidies, or inadequate enforcement. This may include strengthening marine spatial planning, improving fisheries management, reforming pollution control, or enhancing property and resource rights.

4. Sustainability of Conservation Funding:

A common risk is that conservation gains made under a swap erode when earmarked funding ends. Establishing endowment funds, payment-for-ecosystem-services schemes, or integrating conservation spending into core government budgets helps to ensure continuity. Capacity building for local institutions further underpins long-term success.

5. Synergy with International Commitments:

Debt-for-nature swaps should reinforce and accelerate progress toward international agreements, including the SDGs, Aichi Biodiversity Targets, and Paris Agreement goals. Credible links to these frameworks increase access to co-financing, donor support, and technical assistance.

6. Stakeholder Engagement and Social Inclusion:

Long-term sustainability is contingent on the meaningful involvement of communities, Indigenous peoples, women, and other marginalized groups. Policy frameworks should institutionalize participatory governance, fair benefit sharing, and grievance mechanisms to build legitimacy and reduce social risk.

7. Monitoring, Learning, and Adaptation:

Integrated policy alignment requires systems for regular monitoring, evaluation, and adaptive management. This allows for course correction, learning from experience, and continuous improvement of swap design and implementation.

8. Risk Mitigation:

Finally, swaps must be structured to manage risks related to macroeconomic shocks, commodity price fluctuations, and natural disasters, factors particularly acute in small island and coastal economies. Integrating swaps with disaster risk finance, climate insurance, and contingency planning can build resilience.

By ensuring that debt-for-nature swaps are fully aligned with national policy and fiscal frameworks, countries can leverage debt relief not just for short-term conservation wins, but for a sustained transition toward a resilient, inclusive, and sustainable blue economy.

Chapter 5: Public and Multilateral Financial Instruments for Blue Investment

Public and multilateral financial institutions are essential actors in the blue finance ecosystem, providing the catalytic capital, risk mitigation, and technical support required to unlock larger flows of private investment. This chapter examines the full suite of financial instruments, grants, concessional loans, guarantees, credit enhancements, and results-based financing, available from development banks and international financial institutions. It explores programmatic approaches and dedicated funding windows that support integrated marine resilience initiatives and discusses best practices for institutional design and pipeline management. By illustrating how public and multilateral finance can align with national priorities and global sustainability goals, the chapter underscores the importance of partnership and coordination in building a robust blue investment landscape.

Role of Development Banks and International Financial Institutions (IFIs)

Development banks and international financial institutions (IFIs) play a central role in bridging the investment gap for blue finance, catalyzing sustainable ocean projects that might otherwise struggle to attract sufficient funding. Their unique mandates, robust credit ratings, and ability to convene public and private sector actors make them powerful vehicles for scaling up blue investment.

Mandate and Reach:

Multilateral development banks (MDBs), such as the World Bank, Asian Development Bank (ADB), African Development Bank (AfDB), and Inter-American Development Bank (IDB), and regional development finance institutions are mandated to promote sustainable development in member countries. Increasingly, their strategies explicitly reference the blue economy, climate resilience, and biodiversity, signaling a shift toward prioritizing marine and coastal investments alongside more traditional infrastructure and poverty reduction projects.

Risk Appetite and Leverage:

Development banks can provide long-term financing at terms often unavailable from commercial markets, and their involvement serves as a de-risking signal to other investors. This "crowding-in" effect is essential for blue projects, which often feature uncertain returns, regulatory complexity, and high perceived risk. MDBs can also leverage their own resources to unlock multiples of private capital, amplifying the impact of their investments.

Convening Power and Technical Assistance:

Beyond finance, MDBs and IFIs offer valuable technical assistance, policy dialogue, and capacity-building programs to governments and project developers. They support the preparation of investment plans, development of enabling policy frameworks, and mainstreaming of environmental and social safeguards. These activities help build pipelines of bankable projects and ensure alignment with international standards.

Innovative Instruments and Blended Finance:

MDBs are pioneers in developing innovative financial products for the blue economy, such as blue bonds, guarantees, blended finance facilities, and results-based grants. They also act as intermediaries for climate and biodiversity funds (e.g., Global Environment Facility, Green Climate Fund), channeling concessional finance and co-financing to priority marine projects.

Supporting Policy Reform:

Development banks often tie financing to broader policy and governance reforms, such as improving marine spatial planning, reforming fisheries management, or strengthening climate adaptation policies. This policy-based lending approach amplifies the systemic impact of their financial instruments.

Case Examples:

Initiatives such as the World Bank's PROBLUE program and the Asian Development Bank's Healthy Oceans Action Plan illustrate how IFIs are integrating blue economy priorities across operations, combining finance with policy, science, and partnerships.

In summary, development banks and IFIs are essential actors in blue finance, not just as funders but as ecosystem builders, standard-setters, and catalysts for the sustainable transformation of the world's oceans and coasts.

Grants, Concessional Loans, Guarantees, and Credit Enhancements

A wide spectrum of financial instruments, each with its own advantages and challenges, is employed by public agencies and multilateral institutions to mobilize blue finance. Four key types are grants, concessional loans, guarantees, and credit enhancements.

Grants:

Grants remain an essential instrument for early-stage, high-risk, or non-revenue-generating blue projects. These include activities such as scientific research, community-based conservation, policy development, and the establishment of MPAs. Grants provide "catalytic capital," enabling innovation, reducing barriers to market entry, and supporting the creation of enabling environments. Often, grants are paired with technical assistance to build local capacity, develop project pipelines, or test new approaches before scaling.

Concessional Loans:

Concessional loans, also known as "soft loans", are offered at below-market interest rates, with longer maturities and grace periods than commercial loans. These are especially important for developing countries and small island states facing fiscal constraints and limited access to international capital markets. Concessional loans can fund large-scale infrastructure projects (such as wastewater treatment or coastal resilience works), with repayment schedules aligned to project cash flows and socioeconomic benefits.

Guarantees:

Guarantees are risk mitigation instruments that protect investors and lenders against specific risks, such as payment default, political instability, or regulatory changes. Partial risk or credit guarantees from MDBs and bilateral agencies can unlock financing for blue projects that would otherwise be deemed too risky by the private sector. Guarantees may cover debt service, equity investments, or specific project milestones.

Credit Enhancements:

Credit enhancements improve the creditworthiness of a blue project or issuer, lowering the cost of capital and expanding the pool of potential investors. Mechanisms include subordinated debt, reserve funds, first-loss tranches, and insurance products. These instruments are especially effective in blended finance structures, where public funds are used to leverage multiples of private capital.

Blending Instruments for Impact:

Often, these tools are used in combination to maximize leverage and impact. For example, a grant may fund project preparation, a concessional loan may finance capital costs, and a guarantee may protect private lenders, all in a single deal. This layered approach, known as "blended finance," is essential for complex blue economy projects.

Strategic Alignment:

Selecting the appropriate instrument depends on project characteristics, market maturity, and the needs of stakeholders. Multilateral and bilateral donors, as well as philanthropy, play a crucial role in providing flexible, patient capital to unlock larger flows from institutional investors.

Ultimately, this suite of financial instruments expands access to blue finance, aligns incentives across stakeholders, and de-risks investments that are vital for achieving marine conservation, climate adaptation, and sustainable development goals.

Results-Based Financing Models for Ocean Outcomes

Results-based financing (RBF) is a performance-driven approach in which disbursement of funds is directly tied to the achievement of pre-agreed environmental, social, or economic outcomes. In the context of blue finance, RBF models are gaining traction as effective mechanisms for ensuring accountability, incentivizing innovation, and directing resources toward proven interventions in ocean sustainability.

Principles of RBF:

RBF shifts the focus from funding inputs or activities to rewarding outputs, outcomes, or impacts. Payments are only made once verifiable results, such as restored habitats, increased fish stocks, reduced pollution, or improved livelihoods, have been achieved and independently validated. This creates strong incentives for implementers to deliver efficiently and adapt to changing circumstances.

Types of RBF Instruments in Blue Finance:

- **Payment for Ecosystem Services (PES):** Coastal communities, fishers, or landowners are compensated for actions that protect or restore marine ecosystems, such as mangrove replanting or sustainable fisheries management. Payments are contingent on the delivery and maintenance of agreed ecosystem services, like carbon sequestration or improved water quality.
- **Impact Bonds:** Social or environmental impact bonds are outcome-based contracts where private investors provide upfront capital for conservation or resilience interventions. If pre-defined results are achieved, a public agency or donor repays investors with a return; if not, investors bear the risk.
- **Performance-Based Grants or Subsidies:** Grants are structured so that tranches are released based on the achievement of milestones, such as kilometers of coastline restored or the number of communities adopting sustainable practices.
- **Results-Linked Loans:** Concessional loan terms may be improved if performance targets are met, incentivizing borrowers to exceed baseline expectations.

Advantages of RBF in Ocean Finance:

- **Efficiency:** Resources are allocated to the most effective implementers and interventions.
- **Accountability:** Verification and transparency reduce the risk of misallocation or "blue-washing."
- **Scalability:** RBF attracts impact-oriented investors and can crowd in additional capital from those seeking measurable returns.
- **Adaptability:** The model encourages continuous learning, innovation, and adaptation to local contexts.

Challenges and Enabling Conditions:

Implementing RBF in marine contexts requires robust monitoring, reporting, and verification (MRV) systems, often leveraging satellite technology, community science, and third-party audits. It also demands clear definition of outcomes, risk-sharing arrangements, and trust among partners. Capacity building, data infrastructure, and enabling policy environments are key to mainstreaming RBF at scale.

In summary, results-based financing is a critical tool in the blue finance arsenal, driving a shift toward impact, accountability, and efficiency in the pursuit of sustainable ocean outcomes.

Programmatic Approaches and Funding Windows for Marine Resilience

In response to the scale and complexity of ocean and coastal challenges, donors and multilateral agencies increasingly employ programmatic approaches and establish dedicated funding windows for marine resilience. These mechanisms support integrated, multi-project, or multi-country initiatives that are larger in scope, longer in duration, and more strategically aligned than stand-alone projects.

What are Programmatic Approaches?

Programmatic approaches bundle related activities, themes, or geographies into coherent frameworks, such as regional blue economy programs, coastal resilience partnerships, or national adaptation plans. Rather than funding isolated interventions, donors commit resources over several years to a suite of linked projects that share common objectives, governance structures, and performance frameworks.

Dedicated Funding Windows:

Global and regional funds, such as the Green Climate Fund (GCF), Global Environment Facility (GEF), Adaptation Fund, and specialized ocean funds, have established funding windows dedicated to marine and coastal resilience. These windows provide targeted grants, concessional finance, and technical support for priorities such as:

- Marine protected area networks
- Blue carbon and ecosystem restoration
- Coastal infrastructure and nature-based solutions
- Disaster risk reduction and early warning systems
- Fisheries management and sustainable livelihoods

Advantages of Programmatic and Windowed Funding:

- **Scale and Impact:** Bundling resources increases scale, enables transformative interventions, and generates economies of scale in project preparation, implementation, and monitoring.
- **Coherence and Coordination:** Integrated programs ensure alignment with national strategies, policy reform agendas, and global commitments, reducing fragmentation and duplication.
- **Flexibility:** Programmatic funding allows for adaptive management, reallocation of resources, and learning-by-doing over the life of the program.
- **Partnerships:** Larger, multi-stakeholder programs attract a broader array of partners, including governments, communities, NGOs, and the private sector.

Challenges and Enablers:

Successful programmatic approaches require strong governance, clear performance metrics, and effective stakeholder coordination. Institutional capacity for program management, robust MRV systems, and transparent disbursement procedures are critical to maintaining accountability and achieving results.

Examples:

The GCF's "Simplified Approval Process" for smaller-scale adaptation projects, the GEF's International Waters program, and the IDB's Blue Economy Technical Assistance Facility are examples of how programmatic and windowed funding is being operationalized for marine resilience across regions.

By moving beyond piecemeal projects to strategic, program-based approaches, the blue finance community can more effectively build resilience, leverage diverse financing sources, and deliver sustained impact at the scale demanded by global ocean and climate challenges.

Institutional Design for Managing Blue Finance Pipelines

Effective institutional design is a cornerstone of successful blue finance, ensuring that investment pipelines are robust, transparent, and aligned with both national priorities and global standards. Institutions, public agencies, trust funds, development banks, and public-private platforms, are responsible for mobilizing, allocating, and managing resources from diverse sources for the blue economy.

Key Elements of Institutional Design:

- **Clear Mandate and Strategic Alignment:** Institutions managing blue finance must have a clear mandate rooted in national development strategies, blue economy plans, or climate resilience frameworks. Alignment with policy ensures resources are targeted to priority areas and that projects reinforce national and international commitments.
- **Governance and Accountability:** Strong governance structures include independent boards or steering committees, stakeholder representation (including local communities and civil society), and robust internal controls. Transparent decision-making and regular reporting build confidence among donors, investors, and beneficiaries.

- **Pipeline Development and Project Selection:** Institutions need dedicated capacity for pipeline development, including project identification, technical and financial appraisal, and environmental and social screening. Selection criteria should reflect additionality, impact, scalability, and risk.
- **Resource Mobilization:** Effective institutions can attract resources from a wide spectrum of funders, public budgets, grants, MDBs, philanthropy, and private investment. Innovative models, such as endowment funds, revolving funds, or results-based disbursements, expand the financial toolbox.
- **Disbursement and Monitoring:** Institutions must establish efficient, transparent disbursement mechanisms and ensure regular monitoring of both financial flows and project performance. Digital platforms and MRV systems support real-time oversight and adaptive management.
- **Partnerships and Coordination:** Blue finance requires close coordination across sectors, environment, fisheries, infrastructure, finance, and levels of government. Partnerships with MDBs, NGOs, private sector, and communities ensure buy-in, reduce duplication, and increase leverage.
- **Capacity Building:** Investing in staff development, technical training, and institutional learning strengthens long-term effectiveness and sustainability.
- **Safeguards and Risk Management:** Institutions should embed environmental, social, and fiduciary safeguards, as well as systems for grievance redress, to protect against unintended impacts and maintain credibility.

Emerging Best Practices:

Examples of effective institutional design include national blue funds (such as Seychelles Conservation and Climate Adaptation Trust), dedicated blue finance units within ministries, and regional investment platforms. These institutions serve as "one-stop shops" for blue project financing, blending multiple sources and aligning actors around common goals.

In summary, well-designed institutions are the backbone of blue finance pipelines, transforming aspirations into concrete, measurable, and scalable investments that advance marine conservation, climate resilience, and inclusive growth.

Chapter 6: Private Capital and Blended Finance Models

Mobilizing private capital is vital to closing the global investment gap for the sustainable ocean economy. This chapter delves into the evolving role of private investors, ranging from impact funds to institutional asset managers, in financing ocean-related projects and businesses. It unpacks the risk-return profiles of different blue economy sectors, highlighting the specific challenges and opportunities that shape private investment. The chapter provides a comprehensive overview of blended finance models, showing how catalytic capital, risk-sharing, and layered instruments can attract commercial co-investment while safeguarding conservation outcomes. By exploring alignment strategies, investor expectations, and effective de-risking and exit mechanisms, the chapter demonstrates how blended finance can scale impact and mainstream blue investments across markets and geographies.

Role of Private Investors in the Blue Economy

Private investors are becoming an increasingly significant force in advancing the blue economy, helping to close the substantial financing gap left by constrained public budgets and development assistance. As governments and multilateral organizations set ambitious targets for marine conservation, sustainable fisheries, pollution reduction, and coastal resilience, the mobilization of private capital is essential to scale solutions, drive innovation, and deliver measurable impact.

Growing Appetite for Blue Investments

There is growing recognition among institutional investors, such as pension funds, insurance companies, and sovereign wealth funds, of the strategic and financial importance of healthy ocean ecosystems. Marine and coastal assets underpin food security, climate regulation, energy production, and global trade, making the sustainability of the blue economy directly relevant to long-term investment returns. At the same time, impact investors, venture capital, and private equity are seeking opportunities in emerging sectors like sustainable aquaculture, ocean-based renewable energy, marine biotechnology, eco-tourism, and blue carbon.

Drivers of Private Participation

Several factors drive private interest in the blue economy:

- Rising global demand for sustainable seafood and alternative proteins
- Cost competitiveness and scalability of offshore wind, wave, and tidal energy
- Growth of blue carbon markets and nature-based solutions for climate adaptation and mitigation
- Increasing regulatory pressure on supply chains to minimize ocean impacts
- Demand for "green" and "blue" financial products from environmentally conscious consumers and investors

Constraints and Challenges

However, the ocean remains relatively under-invested compared to terrestrial sustainability sectors. Barriers include market fragmentation, limited data and track record, unclear regulatory environments, and the perceived complexity and risk of ocean-related investments. Many blue projects are small-scale or at early stages of commercialization, requiring patient capital and risk tolerance.

The Critical Role of Private Capital

Private capital fills essential gaps in financing, supports the scaling and replication of successful pilots, and injects discipline and innovation into blue sectors. By partnering with public and philanthropic actors, private investors can help structure transactions that leverage grant and concessional finance, de-risk investments, and drive long-term impact. Private investment is also crucial for driving the adoption of new technologies, business models, and market-based solutions, accelerating the transition from extraction to regeneration.

Ultimately, harnessing private capital for the blue economy will determine whether global ambitions for ocean health, climate resilience, and sustainable growth can be achieved at the scale and speed required.

Risk-Return Profiles of Ocean-Related Investments

Understanding the risk-return profile of ocean-related investments is essential for mobilizing private capital at scale. Each segment of the blue economy, fisheries, aquaculture, renewable energy, marine biotechnology, coastal infrastructure, and more, carries its own risk characteristics, return potential, and market dynamics.

Risk Factors Unique to Ocean Investments

- **Environmental Risk:** Projects are exposed to the unpredictability of ocean conditions, climate events (hurricanes, rising sea levels), and ecological shocks (algal blooms, disease outbreaks in aquaculture).
- **Regulatory and Political Risk:** In many jurisdictions, marine resource rights and permitting frameworks are underdeveloped, subject to change, or inconsistently enforced. Policy shifts can affect market access, subsidies, and allowable activities.
- **Market and Demand Risk:** Many blue economy sectors are new or rapidly evolving, with uncertain demand, price volatility, or lack of established off-take agreements.
- **Operational and Technical Risk:** Operating in the marine environment is complex and often costly, ranging from

offshore construction and logistics to ongoing monitoring and maintenance.

- **Reputational and Social Risk:** Ocean projects, such as aquaculture, deep-sea mining, or tourism, are highly visible and may face scrutiny from NGOs, local communities, and media. Poor stakeholder engagement or negative environmental impacts can lead to project delays, protest, or litigation.

Return Potential

- **Mature Sectors:** Infrastructure projects such as offshore wind and port upgrades can deliver stable, long-term returns, especially when backed by government guarantees or regulated tariffs.
- **Emerging Sectors:** Blue carbon, marine biotechnology, and eco-tourism may offer higher risk-adjusted returns for early movers, but with greater uncertainty and longer investment horizons.
- **Impact and Sustainability Premium:** Some investors are willing to accept lower financial returns ("concessionary capital") in exchange for measurable environmental or social impact, particularly in blended finance structures.

Risk Mitigation Strategies

- Diversification across sectors, geographies, and project stages to smooth returns
- Use of risk-sharing mechanisms (insurance, guarantees, first-loss capital)
- Partnering with experienced public, multilateral, or NGO actors for technical due diligence and project development

Evolving Market Dynamics

As the blue finance market matures, increased data availability, standardized metrics, successful track records, and supportive policy frameworks will lower perceived risk, improve pricing, and increase liquidity for ocean investments.

A nuanced understanding of the risk-return landscape, combined with innovative structuring and risk mitigation, will be key to attracting and sustaining private capital flows to the blue economy.

Blended Finance Structures: Catalytic Capital, Risk-Sharing, Layered Instruments

Blended finance is a powerful approach that uses public or philanthropic funds to "crowd in" private capital for sustainable development, particularly in sectors and geographies that might otherwise be seen as too risky or unproven. In the blue economy, blended finance structures are vital for scaling investment, demonstrating new models, and achieving both financial and impact objectives.

What is Blended Finance?

Blended finance combines concessional resources, such as grants, concessional loans, or guarantees, from public, multilateral, or philanthropic actors with commercial investment from private sources. The goal is to improve risk-adjusted returns for private investors and to increase the overall capital available for ocean projects.

Key Components:

- **Catalytic Capital:** Early-stage funding from donors, development banks, or impact funds provides "catalytic" support to prepare projects, test business models, or absorb higher risks. This capital helps develop pipelines and build confidence among commercial investors.
- **Risk-Sharing Mechanisms:** Instruments such as guarantees, insurance, first-loss tranches, and subordinated debt protect

private investors against downside risk, increasing their willingness to participate.

- **Layered Capital Structures:** Funds may be structured in layers, senior, mezzanine, and junior tranches, allowing different investor types to participate according to their risk appetite. Public capital typically takes the most junior position, absorbing first losses to protect senior private investors.

Benefits of Blended Finance in the Blue Economy:

- **Unlocks Scale:** By de-risking projects, blended finance can mobilize large volumes of private capital not otherwise available for blue investments.
- **Builds Markets:** Demonstration projects help establish track records, prove business models, and attract replication.
- **Aligns Incentives:** Allows public and private actors to pursue shared objectives while recognizing their distinct priorities (e.g., impact vs. return).

Examples in the Blue Economy:

- Blue investment funds that blend philanthropic grants with commercial equity and debt for sustainable aquaculture or plastic waste recycling
- Public-private partnerships for offshore wind or coastal infrastructure, with MDBs providing guarantees or concessional loans
- Results-based financing facilities that pay private investors for verifiable improvements in marine biodiversity, fisheries management, or water quality

Challenges:

- Structuring complexity and the need for transparent governance and accountability

- Ensuring that blended finance addresses real market failures and does not subsidize business-as-usual or crowd out private innovation
- Measuring and managing impact alongside financial performance

Enabling Factors:

Clear eligibility and impact criteria, strong MRV systems, supportive legal and regulatory frameworks, and proactive stakeholder engagement

Blended finance is not a panacea, but when well-designed, it can transform the investment landscape for the blue economy, accelerating innovation, scaling solutions, and building markets where none previously existed.

Aligning Private Capital with Conservation Goals

Aligning private investment with conservation outcomes is essential for building a blue economy that is both economically viable and ecologically resilient. While private capital brings needed scale and discipline, it must be intentionally directed to projects and businesses that generate measurable positive impacts for ocean health, biodiversity, and coastal communities.

Defining Conservation Outcomes

Clear, science-based objectives are required to guide private investment toward true conservation gains, rather than inadvertently supporting unsustainable or extractive activities. This means establishing eligibility criteria, performance metrics, and reporting standards that are aligned with international frameworks such as SDG 14, the Paris Agreement, and global biodiversity targets.

Integrating Conservation into Investment Process

- **Screening and Due Diligence:** Investors can require environmental and social impact assessments, as well as ongoing monitoring, as conditions for investment.
- **Green and Blue Taxonomies:** Financial institutions increasingly rely on taxonomies or classification systems to identify activities that qualify as "sustainable" or "blue." These tools help prevent "blue-washing" and provide clarity to investors and issuers.
- **Impact-Linked Financing:** Loans, bonds, or equity may be structured with terms linked to the achievement of conservation targets, such as reducing pollution, protecting habitats, or increasing fish stocks. Failure to meet targets can result in higher interest rates or penalties, while success may trigger bonuses or lower costs.
- **Collaborative Partnerships:** Investors, NGOs, and public agencies can co-design and co-invest in blended structures, leveraging complementary strengths and expertise.
- **Stakeholder Engagement:** Projects that meaningfully engage local communities, Indigenous peoples, and affected stakeholders are more likely to succeed, deliver lasting impact, and reduce social risk.

Innovation and Market-Based Mechanisms

- **Blue Carbon and Ecosystem Services:** Emerging markets for blue carbon credits, habitat banking, and payment for ecosystem services provide new avenues for private investment in restoration and conservation.
- **Insurance and Resilience Products:** Innovative insurance products, such as reef or mangrove insurance, provide incentives for conservation by linking payouts to the health and restoration of natural assets.
- **Certification and Labeling:** Eco-labels for seafood, tourism, or shipping create market demand for sustainable practices and reward conservation-aligned businesses.

Accountability and Transparency

To ensure real impact, investors should commit to transparency, third-party verification, and public reporting on both financial and conservation performance. Standardized ESG and impact disclosure frameworks, such as those developed by the International Finance Corporation (IFC), the Principles for Responsible Investment (PRI), or the Taskforce on Nature-related Financial Disclosures (TNFD), provide useful benchmarks.

By systematically embedding conservation into the DNA of investment strategies, private capital can be a powerful driver of regeneration, ensuring that the growth of the blue economy is compatible with the long-term health of the world's oceans.

Investor Expectations, De-Risking Strategies, and Exit Mechanisms

To attract and retain private investment in the blue economy, it is essential to understand and address investor expectations around risk, return, liquidity, and impact. Purpose-built de-risking strategies and clear exit mechanisms are critical for scaling blue finance.

Investor Expectations in Blue Finance

- **Risk-Adjusted Returns:** Investors seek a balance between acceptable risk and competitive returns, particularly in newer blue sectors lacking deep track records.
- **Impact Performance:** A growing segment of investors, including impact funds, foundations, and ESG-focused asset managers, are motivated by environmental and social impact as well as financial returns. They require robust, verifiable metrics to report results to stakeholders.
- **Liquidity and Exit Options:** Many investors, particularly institutional players, require a clear path to exit their investment within a defined time frame, whether through asset sales, IPOs, refinancing, or secondary markets.
- **Transparency and Governance:** Investors demand transparency on project selection, fund allocation, impact

measurement, and governance. Clear, predictable rules and reporting standards are non-negotiable.

De-Risking Strategies

- **Blended Finance:** As detailed earlier, blending concessional capital with commercial funding allows risk to be shared and mitigated, making projects more attractive to private investors.
- **Insurance Products:** Marine-specific insurance, covering weather, operational, or ecological risk, helps protect revenues and assets, reducing volatility.
- **Guarantees and Credit Enhancements:** Public or multilateral guarantees on loans or bonds reduce credit risk, lower borrowing costs, and improve access to capital markets.
- **Revenue Structures:** Secure off-take agreements, feed-in tariffs, or minimum revenue guarantees for blue infrastructure (such as offshore wind) provide revenue certainty and improve bankability.
- **Portfolio Diversification:** Funds can pool multiple projects, geographies, or sectors to spread risk and increase stability of returns.

Exit Mechanisms

- **Project Sales:** Direct sale of assets (e.g., operational aquaculture farms, wind farms, or eco-resorts) to strategic buyers or infrastructure funds.
- **Refinancing:** Replacement of early-stage capital with lower-cost, long-term debt or equity as projects reach maturity and risk decreases.
- **Public Markets:** IPOs or issuance of asset-backed securities, allowing early investors to realize gains and recycle capital.
- **Secondary Markets:** Growth of a secondary market for blue assets or securities increases liquidity and attracts a wider investor base.

Enabling Conditions

- Strong legal and regulatory frameworks, reliable dispute resolution mechanisms, and government support are essential for investor confidence.
- Ongoing capacity building, pipeline development, and market-making activities by public and philanthropic actors can help "crowd in" private capital at every stage.

In sum, delivering the right mix of de-risking tools and exit strategies will unlock greater flows of private investment, create sustainable blue markets, and ensure that investors can confidently participate in building the future of the ocean economy.

Chapter 7: Governance, Regulation, and Fiduciary Standards

Sound governance, clear regulatory frameworks, and rigorous fiduciary standards are fundamental to the integrity and effectiveness of blue finance. This chapter outlines the legal structures, compliance requirements, and due diligence processes that underpin blue finance eligibility. It details the essentials of fiduciary risk assessment and ongoing monitoring, and explains the critical role of ESG reporting and disclosure in maintaining transparency and trust. The chapter also addresses regulatory advances such as sustainable finance taxonomies and classification systems, and examines the monitoring and enforcement mechanisms required to safeguard against blue-washing. By setting out the governance and regulatory landscape, the chapter equips readers with a blueprint for responsible blue finance management.

Legal Frameworks for Blue Finance Eligibility and Compliance

The integrity, credibility, and long-term success of blue finance depend fundamentally on the strength and clarity of underlying legal frameworks. These frameworks govern which activities and entities qualify for blue finance, establish compliance requirements, and set out enforcement mechanisms to protect both investor interests and environmental outcomes. In a rapidly growing and evolving field, robust legal structures reduce ambiguity, build confidence among market actors, and enable blue finance to deliver on its transformative potential.

Defining Eligibility for Blue Finance

Eligibility frameworks typically draw on international environmental conventions, sustainable finance taxonomies, and national laws to define which projects, activities, or sectors are considered "blue." Legal standards may specify, for example, that only projects with direct, measurable marine or coastal benefits, such as restoration of habitats, sustainable fisheries, or reduction of marine pollution, qualify for blue bonds or loans. Activities that risk significant environmental harm or fall outside accepted sustainability criteria are explicitly excluded.

Legal Requirements for Issuers and Investors

For issuers (such as governments, corporations, or multilateral institutions), legal frameworks impose obligations to disclose the use of proceeds, ensure funds are ring-fenced for eligible activities, and provide for regular impact reporting. For investors, laws may mandate due diligence on environmental and social risk, compliance with anti-money laundering (AML) and counter-terrorist financing (CTF) provisions, and adherence to "know your customer" (KYC) rules. These requirements safeguard market integrity and guard against reputational and financial risk.

International and National Harmonization

Legal frameworks for blue finance are increasingly harmonized across borders, drawing on standards from the International Capital Market Association (ICMA), the European Union's Sustainable Finance Disclosure Regulation (SFDR), and guidance from the Taskforce on Nature-related Financial Disclosures (TNFD). At the national level, countries may enact blue economy strategies, marine spatial planning laws, or environmental protection acts that set parameters for blue investment. Alignment between international and domestic law enhances predictability and facilitates cross-border capital flows.

Enforcement and Legal Remedies

Enforcement provisions may include penalties for misreporting, contractual remedies for non-compliance, and rights for investors or regulators to audit use of proceeds. Clear dispute resolution mechanisms, arbitration, mediation, or recourse to courts, are essential, especially for cross-jurisdictional transactions.

Adapting to Evolving Science and Practice

As scientific understanding of marine ecosystems, climate risks, and sustainable practices evolves, legal frameworks must remain flexible and responsive. Mechanisms for regular review, stakeholder consultation, and amendment are vital to ensure that blue finance keeps pace with emerging risks, opportunities, and best practices.

Ultimately, robust legal frameworks underpin the trust required for blue finance to thrive, ensuring investments are directed where they are most needed and safeguarding both financial returns and ocean health.

Fiduciary Risk Assessment and Due Diligence in Marine Finance

Fiduciary risk assessment and due diligence are central to the prudent management of blue finance. In this context, fiduciary responsibility refers to the legal and ethical obligation of asset managers, fund trustees, banks, and project sponsors to act in the best interests of their beneficiaries or stakeholders. Effective risk management protects against financial loss, fraud, misallocation of resources, and reputational damage, while ensuring that funds are used as intended to generate measurable marine and social benefits.

Fiduciary Risk in the Blue Context

The blue economy presents specific fiduciary risks, including the complexity of marine projects, fluctuating environmental conditions, regulatory uncertainty, and limited historical data on project performance. Potential risks include:

- Misuse or diversion of funds

- Failure to achieve stated environmental or social objectives
- Cost overruns or project delays due to technical or logistical challenges
- Legal disputes over resource rights or regulatory approvals

Due Diligence Processes

Due diligence is a structured process through which all material aspects of a project or investment are assessed prior to commitment. Key elements include:

- **Legal Due Diligence:** Verification of project ownership, rights to marine and coastal resources, compliance with permits and licenses, and alignment with relevant laws and regulations.
- **Financial Due Diligence:** Analysis of project budgets, funding sources, revenue streams, and assumptions underlying financial models.
- **Technical Due Diligence:** Assessment of project design, technology choices, environmental impacts, and operational feasibility.
- **Social and Environmental Due Diligence:** Evaluation of potential impacts on communities, Indigenous peoples, biodiversity, and ecosystem services; confirmation of stakeholder consultation and social license to operate.

Risk Assessment Tools and Methodologies

Institutions may use a range of tools to quantify and manage fiduciary risk, such as risk registers, probability-impact matrices, stress testing, and scenario analysis. Insurance and hedging products can be deployed to transfer or mitigate specific risks.

Ongoing Monitoring and Compliance

Fiduciary risk management does not end at financial close. Ongoing monitoring, periodic audits, and adaptive management are essential for early detection of emerging risks and ensuring compliance with covenants and impact targets.

Role of Independent Assurance

External auditors, independent evaluation agencies, and third-party verifiers provide additional layers of assurance for stakeholders. Their findings support continuous improvement, inform corrective actions, and build market confidence.

Alignment with International Best Practice

The adoption of internationally recognized frameworks, such as the Equator Principles, IFC Performance Standards, and OECD Guidelines for Multinational Enterprises, ensures that fiduciary standards in blue finance meet global expectations.

In sum, diligent fiduciary risk assessment is not just a legal requirement but a market necessity, supporting the integrity, credibility, and long-term success of blue finance.

ESG Reporting, Disclosure, and Verification in the Ocean Context

ESG reporting, disclosure, and verification are vital pillars of blue finance, providing transparency and accountability to investors, regulators, and society. In the marine context, ESG frameworks are tailored to reflect the specific characteristics, risks, and opportunities associated with ocean and coastal investments.

Purpose and Benefits of ESG Reporting

Comprehensive ESG disclosure:

- Allows investors to evaluate the sustainability and risk profile of their blue investments
- Builds trust with stakeholders, including communities, regulators, and civil society
- Supports compliance with legal requirements and voluntary standards
- Enables benchmarking, learning, and continuous improvement

Key ESG Metrics for Blue Finance

- **Environmental:** Area (km^2) of marine habitats protected or restored, levels of marine pollution prevented or reduced, sustainable fish stock management, carbon sequestration via blue carbon ecosystems, water quality indicators.
- **Social:** Jobs created in sustainable blue sectors, inclusion of marginalized or Indigenous groups, stakeholder engagement processes, gender equality metrics, social benefit-sharing.
- **Governance:** Board and management diversity, transparency in project selection and fund allocation, anti-corruption measures, community representation in governance, grievance mechanisms.

Disclosure Requirements and Best Practices

- **Periodic Reporting:** Issuers of blue bonds or funds are typically required to provide annual or semi-annual ESG reports, detailing the allocation of proceeds, project progress, and impact achieved.
- **Standardization:** Adoption of recognized reporting standards, such as the Global Reporting Initiative (GRI), Sustainability Accounting Standards Board (SASB), or ICMA's Blue Bond Principles, enables comparability and aggregation across projects and issuers.
- **Materiality and Relevance:** Reporting focuses on issues that are material to the marine context and of concern to investors and stakeholders, ensuring information is decision-useful.

Verification and Assurance

- **Third-Party Assurance:** Independent audits, site visits, and verification of reported outcomes provide credibility and reduce the risk of "blue-washing."
- **Certification Schemes:** Participation in certification programs (e.g., Marine Stewardship Council, Aquaculture Stewardship Council, or Verified Carbon Standard for blue carbon) signals commitment to high ESG standards.

Digital Tools and Transparency

The use of digital platforms, satellite monitoring, and blockchain technology is increasing in blue finance ESG disclosure. These tools enhance traceability, accessibility, and real-time verification of data.

Challenges and Next Steps

Despite progress, challenges remain: data gaps, lack of standardization for some metrics, and the cost of verification for smaller issuers. Ongoing international cooperation is needed to further harmonize ESG reporting and ensure small-scale projects are not left behind.

High-quality ESG disclosure is non-negotiable for the credibility and scalability of blue finance, and essential for mainstreaming ocean investments within global capital markets.

Regulatory Frameworks Supporting Blue Finance (Taxonomies, Classification Systems)

The development and implementation of regulatory frameworks, including taxonomies and classification systems, are transforming the landscape of blue finance. These frameworks provide much-needed clarity, consistency, and confidence to issuers, investors, and regulators regarding what qualifies as "blue," how risks are managed, and what standards of conduct and reporting are required.

The Purpose of Taxonomies in Blue Finance

A taxonomy is a structured system for classifying economic activities and investments according to their environmental sustainability. In the blue context, taxonomies help prevent "blue-washing", the misleading labelling of financial products as sustainable without real marine or social benefits. They enable the alignment of financial flows with science-based targets, global commitments, and regulatory requirements.

International and Regional Initiatives

- **European Union:** The EU Taxonomy for Sustainable Activities is pioneering, including criteria for several blue economy sectors (such as fisheries, shipping, and marine renewable energy). While not yet comprehensive for all marine activities, it sets a template for others to follow.
- **ASEAN and National Taxonomies:** Regional groupings and countries such as Singapore, Indonesia, and Seychelles are developing or piloting blue finance taxonomies to align with their specific marine contexts and policy priorities.
- **Global Initiatives:** The International Capital Market Association (ICMA), the UN Environment Programme Finance Initiative (UNEP FI), and the Taskforce on Nature-related Financial Disclosures (TNFD) are shaping global best practice and guidance for classification and disclosure.

Classification Criteria

Taxonomies establish technical screening criteria for eligible activities, minimum safeguards, and "do no significant harm" requirements. For example, a blue taxonomy may define sustainable aquaculture in terms of stocking density, feed sourcing, waste management, and community engagement. Shipping investments may be classified based on emissions reduction, ballast water treatment, and adherence to international maritime conventions.

Regulatory Integration

Financial regulators are beginning to require banks, asset managers, and institutional investors to assess and disclose the alignment of their portfolios with sustainable and blue taxonomies. This drives market discipline, enhances investor confidence, and encourages a shift in capital allocation toward ocean-positive activities.

Challenges in Implementation

- Ensuring that taxonomies are science-based, credible, and adaptable to emerging knowledge
- Balancing inclusivity and ambition, particularly for developing countries and small-scale actors
- Avoiding excessive complexity or compliance costs that could deter participation

The Way Forward

Further development and international harmonization of blue finance taxonomies will be essential to scale investment, improve impact measurement, and support regulatory supervision. Public-private dialogue, iterative refinement, and capacity building will be required to ensure that taxonomies support both market growth and environmental integrity.

Well-crafted regulatory frameworks and taxonomies are indispensable tools for channeling finance to genuine blue economy activities, safeguarding against abuse, and supporting a resilient ocean finance ecosystem.

Monitoring and Enforcement Mechanisms

Effective monitoring and enforcement are foundational to the credibility and success of blue finance. These mechanisms ensure that investments deliver on their intended environmental, social, and economic outcomes, and that issuers, project developers, and fund managers are held accountable for compliance with legal, regulatory, and voluntary standards.

Components of Monitoring in Blue Finance

- **Performance Monitoring:** Regular collection, analysis, and reporting of data on key performance indicators (KPIs) for funded activities. This includes tracking ecological metrics (e.g., habitat restoration, biodiversity gains), financial flows, community benefits, and progress against milestones.
- **Compliance Monitoring:** Ongoing assessment of whether issuers and projects adhere to eligibility criteria, use of proceeds, legal covenants, and ESG reporting obligations.
- **Environmental and Social Safeguards:** Monitoring the implementation of safeguards to prevent negative impacts, such as displacement of communities, harm to vulnerable species, or unintended ecosystem degradation.

Tools and Techniques

- **Digital and Remote Sensing:** Advances in satellite imagery, drones, and environmental sensors enable near real-time monitoring of marine environments, compliance with spatial boundaries (e.g., marine protected areas), and detection of illegal activities.
- **Third-Party Verification and Audits:** Independent auditors or evaluation agencies are often engaged to verify self-reported data, conduct site visits, and assess the credibility of impact claims.
- **Community and Stakeholder Monitoring:** Participatory monitoring involving local communities, fishers, and NGOs strengthens social legitimacy, leverages local knowledge, and increases early detection of problems.

Enforcement Mechanisms

- **Contractual Remedies:** Legal agreements specify remedies for non-compliance, such as suspension of payments, clawback of funds, acceleration of loan repayments, or penalties for misreporting.
- **Regulatory Enforcement:** Supervisory agencies may investigate complaints, impose fines, or revoke licenses or eligibility for future blue finance instruments.
- **Disclosure and Transparency:** Public reporting of monitoring outcomes creates reputational incentives for compliance and enables market discipline.

Grievance and Redress Mechanisms

Accessible mechanisms for stakeholders to raise concerns or report violations are essential for transparency and fairness. This may include ombudspersons, hotlines, or structured feedback channels.

Adaptive Management and Continuous Improvement

Monitoring and enforcement are not static; they support learning, adaptation, and improvement. Feedback loops allow project designs, governance, and standards to evolve in response to emerging challenges, data, or stakeholder input.

Building Capacity

Investing in institutional and technical capacity for monitoring, verification, and enforcement is especially important in low-resource or high-risk settings. Donor support, technical assistance, and knowledge sharing play key roles in building durable systems.

Robust monitoring and enforcement safeguard against "blue-washing," support trust and market growth, and ultimately ensure that blue finance fulfills its promise of delivering real, measurable, and lasting benefits for people and planet.

Chapter 8: Measurement, Impact, and Accountability Frameworks

Measuring and demonstrating real-world impact is at the core of credible blue finance. This chapter presents the frameworks, indicators, and metrics used to track environmental, social, and economic outcomes for blue investments. It details how performance is assessed in terms of biodiversity, ecosystem services, carbon, and livelihoods, and underscores the value of third-party verification and certification in assuring results. The chapter explores the integration of local, Indigenous, and community perspectives in measurement systems, ensuring that outcomes are meaningful and inclusive. It concludes by highlighting the importance of adaptive management and continuous learning, essential for keeping pace with evolving science, technology, and stakeholder expectations in ocean finance.

Key Performance Indicators for Blue Finance

The credibility and effectiveness of blue finance rely on robust, transparent, and relevant performance measurement systems. Key performance indicators (KPIs) are the foundational tools used to track progress, assess results, and ensure accountability for investments in the blue economy. For blue finance, KPIs must reflect both the unique characteristics of marine and coastal systems and the diverse set of environmental, social, and economic outcomes that investors and stakeholders expect.

Defining Effective KPIs for Blue Finance

Effective KPIs are:

- **Specific:** Clearly tied to the objectives of the investment and easy to interpret.
- **Measurable:** Based on quantitative or qualitative data that can be reliably collected.

- **Achievable:** Realistic given the context, resources, and timeframe.
- **Relevant:** Meaningful to the stakeholders and linked to marine sustainability goals.
- **Time-bound:** Structured to track progress over defined periods.

Core KPI Categories in Blue Finance

- **Environmental KPIs:** These measure changes in marine ecosystem health, pollution reduction, habitat restoration, and sustainable use of natural resources. Examples include hectares of restored mangroves, reductions in plastic waste entering oceans, or improvements in water quality.
- **Social KPIs:** Focused on community wellbeing, equity, and inclusion, such as the number of jobs created in blue sectors, proportion of women employed, or levels of community participation in governance.
- **Economic KPIs:** Related to financial viability, return on investment, cost savings, or value generated through sustainable blue economy activities.
- **Governance KPIs:** Indicators that track transparency, stakeholder engagement, compliance with reporting standards, or the establishment of grievance mechanisms.

Setting Baselines and Targets

KPIs are most valuable when they are compared against credible baselines (pre-investment or pre-intervention conditions) and progress is measured toward defined targets. Baseline studies, participatory needs assessments, and expert input help set realistic and meaningful starting points.

Data Sources and Frequency

Sources for KPI data can include field surveys, remote sensing, administrative records, community reporting, and financial disclosures. Monitoring frequency varies by indicator but should be sufficient to capture meaningful change and inform adaptive management.

Transparency and Accessibility

Public reporting on KPIs, through annual reports, digital dashboards, or stakeholder meetings, supports transparency, trust, and market discipline. Investors, regulators, and communities alike benefit from accessible and understandable performance information.

Evolving and Harmonizing KPIs

As the blue finance field matures, efforts are underway to harmonize KPIs across projects and issuers, enabling aggregation, benchmarking, and comparability. International initiatives, such as the International Capital Market Association (ICMA) Blue Bond Principles and the Global Reporting Initiative (GRI), are providing guidance to standardize metrics in the marine context.

In sum, well-designed KPIs are the linchpin of effective blue finance measurement, providing the evidence base required for accountability, learning, and continual improvement.

Metrics for Biodiversity, Ecosystem Services, Livelihoods, and Carbon

Metrics are the specific quantitative and qualitative measures that underpin each KPI. In blue finance, metrics must capture the complexity of ocean ecosystems, the services they provide, and the interdependence of environmental, economic, and social systems.

Biodiversity Metrics

Biodiversity is a critical indicator of ecosystem health and resilience. Blue finance metrics may include:

- **Species richness and abundance:** Number of species and individuals present in a given area before and after intervention.
- **Population trends:** Status of endangered or commercially valuable species, including fish stock assessments.
- **Habitat extent and connectivity:** Area (hectares or square kilometers) of coral reefs, seagrass beds, mangroves, or other critical habitats restored or protected.
- **Invasive species control:** Reduction in populations of harmful non-native species.

Ecosystem Services Metrics

Healthy marine ecosystems provide a host of services that support human and planetary wellbeing. Key metrics include:

- **Coastal protection:** Reduction in coastal erosion or flood risk due to restored mangroves or reefs.
- **Water filtration:** Improvements in water quality attributed to wetland or oyster reef restoration.
- **Nursery functions:** Enhancement of fish recruitment and biomass due to protected nursery habitats.
- **Blue carbon:** Carbon sequestration rates in coastal ecosystems, often measured in tonnes of CO_2-equivalent per hectare per year.

Livelihood Metrics

Sustainable blue finance must deliver tangible benefits to people, especially those most dependent on the ocean. Metrics may track:

- **Income generation:** Changes in household income from blue economy activities (e.g., sustainable fishing, aquaculture, tourism).

- **Job creation:** Number of new jobs or businesses started in targeted sectors.
- **Access to markets:** Number of community members accessing certified sustainable supply chains.
- **Capacity building:** Number of people trained or new skills developed through financed projects.

Carbon Metrics

Marine and coastal ecosystems are increasingly recognized for their carbon storage and sequestration potential, vital for climate mitigation:

- **Blue carbon stock:** Total carbon stored in seagrasses, mangroves, salt marshes, and sediments.
- **Emissions avoided:** Reduction in greenhouse gas emissions from marine renewable energy, modal shifts in shipping, or reduced fertilizer use.

Selecting and Customizing Metrics

Not all metrics are relevant for every project. Selection depends on the goals, context, and scale of the investment. Where possible, metrics should align with recognized international standards (such as IPBES for biodiversity or the Verified Carbon Standard for carbon).

Aggregation and Reporting

Combining metrics across projects enables portfolio-level reporting, benchmarking, and aggregation of impact at scale, a growing demand from institutional investors and regulators.

Metrics for biodiversity, ecosystem services, livelihoods, and carbon together provide a comprehensive view of the real-world outcomes of blue finance, supporting both accountability and adaptive management.

Role of Third-Party Verification and Certification

Independent third-party verification and certification are fundamental to the credibility, transparency, and market acceptance of blue finance. These mechanisms assure investors, regulators, and the public that reported outcomes are real, additional, and consistent with established standards.

Why Third-Party Verification Matters

- **Credibility:** Independent verification mitigates risks of "blue-washing", the overstatement or misrepresentation of environmental or social impact.
- **Investor Confidence:** Capital providers, especially institutional investors, demand assurances that funds are used as intended and outcomes are measured reliably.
- **Market Integrity:** Verification upholds standards across the sector, creating a level playing field for issuers and project developers.

Types of Verification and Certification

- **External Audits:** Financial and impact audits are conducted by accredited third parties, reviewing financial records, data collection processes, and outcome reporting.
- **On-Site Assessments:** Independent verifiers may conduct field visits, stakeholder interviews, and technical reviews to confirm implementation and impact.

- **Certification Schemes:** Voluntary or mandatory certification programs provide recognized "seals of approval" for projects or products. In blue finance, examples include:

  - **Marine Stewardship Council (MSC):** Certification for sustainable wild-capture fisheries.
  - **Aquaculture Stewardship Council (ASC):** Certification for responsible aquaculture.

o **Verified Carbon Standard (VCS):** Certification for blue carbon projects.
o **Blue Bonds Principles:** Issuers may seek certification of bond frameworks by recognized standard-setters.

Process of Verification

- **Design and Pre-Issuance:** Verification of project eligibility, impact frameworks, and alignment with relevant taxonomies or standards.
- **Implementation and Monitoring:** Ongoing review of project execution, data collection, and outcome delivery.
- **Post-Implementation:** Evaluation of achieved outcomes, lessons learned, and compliance with covenants.

Challenges and Considerations

- **Cost:** Verification and certification can be costly, especially for small-scale projects or issuers.
- **Data Availability:** Verification depends on the availability, quality, and granularity of data.
- **Capacity:** Both verifiers and project implementers require technical capacity and up-to-date knowledge.

Evolving Standards

As the blue finance field matures, standards for verification and certification are evolving, with greater emphasis on harmonization, interoperability, and digital verification (e.g., blockchain for traceability).

Regulatory Trends

Some jurisdictions and exchanges are making third-party verification mandatory for certain blue finance instruments, particularly for bonds or large-scale funds.

Market Advantage

Projects and issuers with credible third-party verification and certification may enjoy preferential access to finance, lower cost of capital, and enhanced reputation.

In conclusion, third-party verification and certification are key safeguards in blue finance, providing the assurance needed to grow the market, attract investment, and drive real impact for oceans and communities.

Integrating Local, Indigenous, and Community Outcomes

The effectiveness and legitimacy of blue finance depend on the meaningful integration of local, Indigenous, and community outcomes throughout project and investment lifecycles. Coastal and Indigenous peoples are often the stewards of marine environments and the most directly affected by ocean finance activities. Their participation, rights, and priorities must be central to measurement, impact, and accountability frameworks.

Principles for Integration

- **Free, Prior, and Informed Consent (FPIC):** Projects should respect Indigenous and community rights to participate in decision-making about the use of marine and coastal resources.
- **Co-Design and Co-Management:** Involving local actors in the design, governance, and monitoring of blue finance projects improves relevance, buy-in, and outcomes.
- **Equitable Benefit-Sharing:** Investments should provide tangible, fair, and culturally appropriate benefits to local communities, including employment, infrastructure, profit-sharing, and capacity-building.

Community-Driven Metrics and Indicators

Metrics should reflect the priorities and knowledge of local communities. Examples include:

- **Traditional knowledge indicators:** Recognition of Indigenous ecological knowledge in setting baselines and monitoring changes.
- **Cultural and spiritual values:** Incorporation of sites and practices of cultural importance in impact assessments.
- **Community-defined outcomes:** Jobs created for local youth, increased food security, restoration of traditional fisheries, or enhanced community resilience.

Participatory Monitoring and Evaluation

Community-led data collection, monitoring, and evaluation build capacity, empower local actors, and improve the quality and credibility of results. Mobile technology, citizen science, and partnerships with local organizations can facilitate participatory approaches.

Addressing Social Risks and Conflicts

Strong grievance mechanisms, transparent communication, and ongoing consultation reduce the risk of social conflict, marginalization, or unintended harm.

Institutionalizing Integration

Formal representation of local and Indigenous stakeholders in project governance bodies, advisory panels, and funding allocation decisions ensures ongoing participation and influence.

Policy and Regulatory Support

National and international legal frameworks increasingly recognize the rights of Indigenous and local communities in ocean governance (e.g., the UN Declaration on the Rights of Indigenous Peoples, Convention on Biological Diversity). Blue finance projects should align with these frameworks and exceed minimum standards.

Success Stories and Learning

Examples from around the world demonstrate that community-driven blue finance projects are often more sustainable, adaptive, and resilient, delivering broader social and environmental impact.

By centering local, Indigenous, and community outcomes, blue finance not only delivers better results for people and planet but also builds the social license and legitimacy required for long-term success.

Adaptive Management and Learning in Finance Design

Oceans and coastal systems are dynamic and unpredictable, requiring blue finance to embrace adaptive management and continuous learning. Adaptive management is an iterative approach to decision-making in the face of uncertainty, grounded in monitoring, evaluation, and flexible course correction. In blue finance, embedding adaptive management ensures that investments remain effective and resilient as conditions evolve.

Principles of Adaptive Management

- **Iterative Planning:** Finance design and project implementation proceed in cycles of planning, action, monitoring, evaluation, and adjustment.
- **Evidence-Based Decision-Making:** Real-time data, stakeholder feedback, and scientific research inform ongoing decision-making.

- **Flexibility:** Financing instruments, project activities, and governance structures are designed to accommodate change, whether driven by new knowledge, environmental shifts, or stakeholder priorities.

Integrating Adaptive Management into Blue Finance

- **Feedback Loops:** Monitoring and evaluation systems feed back into project planning, allowing for timely modifications.
- **Contingency Funds and Triggers:** Finance design may include contingency reserves or predefined triggers for reallocation, scaling up, or course correction.
- **Scenario Analysis and Stress Testing:** Anticipating a range of possible futures helps identify risks and prepare responsive strategies.
- **Collaborative Learning:** Multi-stakeholder platforms foster joint problem-solving, knowledge exchange, and sharing of lessons learned.

Institutional and Cultural Factors

Adaptive management requires a culture of learning, openness to failure, and incentives for innovation. Institutions managing blue finance must invest in staff training, organizational learning, and partnerships with research organizations and communities.

Enabling Technologies

Digital tools, data analytics, and remote sensing enable more rapid, granular, and responsive management. Online platforms can disseminate results, lessons, and best practices to a global audience.

Policy and Governance Alignment

Legal and regulatory frameworks should recognize and enable adaptive management, providing flexibility in funding agreements, reporting schedules, and project milestones.

Benefits of Adaptive Finance

- **Increased Effectiveness:** Ability to respond to changing conditions, emerging threats, or new opportunities increases impact.
- **Risk Management:** Early identification and management of problems reduces losses and maximizes returns.
- **Resilience:** Adaptive approaches build resilience into both natural systems and financial structures, making blue finance more robust to shocks.

Challenges

Potential barriers include institutional inertia, rigid donor or investor requirements, and lack of capacity or data. Overcoming these requires committed leadership and sustained investment in learning.

In conclusion, adaptive management and learning are essential for navigating the complexity and change inherent in ocean systems, ensuring that blue finance delivers meaningful, lasting, and resilient impact.

Chapter 9: Scaling Blue Finance Through Innovation and Policy Alignment

Scaling blue finance to meet the ambitions of global ocean sustainability requires innovation in both financial instruments and policy frameworks. This chapter surveys the latest advances, such as tokenized blue finance, digital platforms, and crowdfunding, and shows how these tools are broadening access and driving efficiency. It examines how robust project pipelines are built and maintained, and how national and regional policy frameworks can align capital with blue economy goals. The chapter also highlights the strategic importance of national ocean finance plans and marine spatial planning, and outlines future directions for mainstreaming blue finance across markets and sectors. By connecting innovation with enabling policy, the chapter maps a pathway for scaling impact and transforming the ocean finance landscape.

Innovation in Financial Instruments (Tokenized Blue Finance, Digital Platforms)

Innovation in financial instruments is accelerating the growth and scalability of blue finance, unlocking new sources of capital, improving efficiency, and enhancing transparency in the allocation and tracking of funds. As the demand for sustainable investment rises, the emergence of digital tools and novel financial structures, such as tokenized assets, blockchain-powered platforms, and fintech-enabled blue finance products, offers both opportunities and challenges for the ocean finance ecosystem.

Tokenized Blue Finance

Tokenization refers to the digital representation of ownership or value, such as shares, debt, or even ecosystem services, on a blockchain or distributed ledger. In blue finance, tokenization enables the fractionalization of large investments, making it possible for a wider range of investors (including retail and impact investors) to participate in projects previously accessible only to institutional players. Examples include:

- **Tokenized blue bonds or loans** that are tradeable in small units and settled transparently through smart contracts, reducing transaction costs and increasing liquidity.
- **Digital blue carbon credits** that are traceable and verifiable, enabling companies and individuals to invest directly in the restoration and preservation of seagrasses, mangroves, or other marine carbon sinks.

Blockchain and Digital Platforms

Blockchain technology offers immutable, transparent, and tamper-resistant records of transactions, which is invaluable for tracking impact, preventing fraud, and ensuring that funds are used as intended. Digital platforms can facilitate:

- **Direct investment into blue projects**, with end-to-end traceability of how funds are allocated and what results are achieved.
- **Automated monitoring and reporting**, using integrated IoT sensors, satellite data, and real-time dashboards to provide continuous updates to investors and stakeholders.
- **Smart contracts** that automatically trigger payments or release of funds upon verification of milestones or achievement of impact targets.

Crowdfunding and Peer-to-Peer Models

Digital innovation is also democratizing blue finance through crowdfunding platforms, where communities, NGOs, and entrepreneurs can raise capital from a global audience for marine restoration, plastic removal, or eco-tourism ventures. Peer-to-peer lending platforms match small-scale blue projects with lenders who seek impact alongside returns.

Opportunities and Challenges

- **Opportunities:** Increased access to capital, greater inclusion of small investors, enhanced transparency, faster settlement, and lower transaction costs.
- **Challenges:** Regulatory uncertainty, cybersecurity risks, lack of standardized protocols, and the need for digital literacy among project sponsors and communities.

The Road Ahead

As these innovations mature, collaboration among technologists, financiers, policymakers, and local actors will be essential to ensure digital tools are used responsibly and inclusively. Standards, best practices, and robust governance will be key to harnessing innovation for genuine and equitable progress in blue finance.

Building Pipelines of Bankable Ocean Projects

A well-developed pipeline of bankable projects is critical for scaling blue finance and ensuring that available capital translates into meaningful impact on ocean health and livelihoods. The persistent lack of investable, scalable, and commercially viable blue projects remains one of the main obstacles to deploying finance at the pace and scale required by global ocean and climate goals.

Defining "Bankable" in the Blue Economy

Bankable projects are those that meet the technical, financial, environmental, and social criteria demanded by investors, lenders, and donors. They must demonstrate:

- A clear business model and revenue streams
- Legal rights and permits to operate
- Robust environmental and social safeguards

- Capacity for measurement, reporting, and verification (MRV) of impact
- Governance and management structures that ensure transparency and accountability

Challenges in Project Pipeline Development

- **Early-Stage Barriers:** Many blue economy projects, particularly in developing countries or small island states, lack the technical expertise, financial resources, or market access required to move from concept to investment-ready status.
- **Scale and Aggregation:** Numerous small-scale or community-based projects struggle to attract commercial investment due to their size, risk, or lack of track record. Aggregation platforms or funds can bundle multiple small projects into investable vehicles.
- **Data and Feasibility:** Limited availability of baseline data, feasibility studies, and impact assessments hinders project preparation and due diligence.
- **Capacity Constraints:** Government agencies, NGOs, and entrepreneurs may require technical assistance and capacity building to design, finance, and manage projects to international standards.

Solutions and Best Practices

- **Technical Assistance Facilities:** Development banks and donors increasingly offer project preparation facilities, providing grant funding and expert support for feasibility studies, business planning, environmental impact assessments, and structuring deals.
- **Blended Finance Vehicles:** These can absorb higher risk, provide patient capital, and attract commercial co-investors once projects are de-risked.
- **Pipeline Platforms:** Digital and physical platforms, such as blue project registries and match-making events, connect

project developers with investors, technical partners, and knowledge resources.

- **Standardized Documentation:** Developing standardized templates for contracts, impact measurement, and reporting can reduce transaction costs and accelerate project development.
- **Capacity Building and Mentorship:** Partnerships with academic institutions, multilateral organizations, and established businesses can build local skills and foster innovation.

Enabling Environment

Strong government commitment, clear regulatory frameworks, and policies supporting innovation and entrepreneurship are foundational for building robust project pipelines.

Conclusion

By systematically developing, aggregating, and de-risking blue economy projects, stakeholders can unleash a flow of investment that delivers real-world benefits for oceans, people, and climate.

National and Regional Policy Frameworks to Align Finance with Blue Economy Goals

Policy alignment is one of the most powerful levers for scaling blue finance. National and regional frameworks provide the enabling conditions for investment, ensuring that public and private capital flows toward activities that advance marine sustainability, economic resilience, and social inclusion.

The Role of Policy in Blue Finance

- **Clarity and Predictability:** Clear policies give investors confidence that rules will not change abruptly, reduce regulatory risk, and foster long-term planning.
- **Priority Setting:** National and regional blue economy strategies define priority sectors (e.g., sustainable fisheries, blue carbon, marine renewable energy), target investment gaps, and set measurable goals for impact.
- **Integration with Broader Agendas:** Effective frameworks link blue finance to broader economic, climate, and development policies, such as Nationally Determined Contributions (NDCs) under the Paris Agreement, biodiversity action plans, or disaster risk reduction strategies.
- **Incentives and Regulation:** Tax incentives, subsidies, preferential lending, or fast-track permitting can catalyze blue investments, while regulations can set minimum sustainability standards and penalties for non-compliance.

Regional Approaches

Regional frameworks, such as the Caribbean's Blue Economy Framework, the African Union's Agenda 2063, or ASEAN's blue finance initiatives, help harmonize standards, pool resources, and foster cross-border cooperation. Regional development banks and multilateral platforms can scale finance for transboundary marine issues, such as migratory species protection, pollution control, and climate adaptation.

Examples of Enabling Policies

- **Marine Spatial Planning (MSP):** Policies that allocate ocean space to different uses, fishing, tourism, conservation, energy, create clarity and reduce conflict.
- **Blue Bond Guidelines:** National guidance on blue bond issuance ensures that proceeds are directed to eligible, high-impact activities.

- **Legal Recognition of Blue Carbon:** By recognizing the value of blue carbon in national GHG inventories, countries can unlock finance through carbon markets or climate funds.

Public-Private Dialogue

Ongoing consultation between governments, investors, communities, and civil society ensures that frameworks remain relevant, ambitious, and inclusive. Policy platforms, taskforces, and advisory committees provide avenues for coordination and feedback.

Monitoring, Evaluation, and Learning

Regular assessment of policy impacts, transparency in reporting, and willingness to adapt frameworks over time are hallmarks of effective policy alignment.

Conclusion

Well-designed policy frameworks underpin investor confidence, unlock new sources of capital, and align national and regional development with global sustainability imperatives for the ocean.

Role of National Ocean Finance Plans and Marine Spatial Planning

Strategic planning tools such as national ocean finance plans and MSP are essential for operationalizing blue economy ambitions and ensuring that finance is directed efficiently, equitably, and sustainably.

National Ocean Finance Plans

A national ocean finance plan is a government-led strategy that identifies priority investment needs, sources of finance, implementation pathways, and measurable outcomes for the blue economy. These plans:

- **Diagnose Investment Gaps:** Assess where funding shortfalls exist, be it in conservation, infrastructure, climate adaptation, or livelihoods.
- **Map Sources and Instruments:** Align public budgets, donor resources, private investment, and innovative financial instruments (such as blue bonds, debt swaps, or blended finance) with priority actions.
- **Sequence and Coordinate Investments:** Provide a roadmap for investment sequencing, ensuring that foundational activities (e.g., policy reform, capacity building) precede or accompany larger financial flows.
- **Leverage Partnerships:** Facilitate partnerships across government, private sector, development agencies, and civil society for co-investment, co-management, and joint learning.

MSP

MSP is the process of analyzing and allocating ocean space for different uses to reduce conflicts, promote efficiency, and protect marine ecosystems. Well-implemented MSP:

- **Enables Coexistence:** Facilitates balance between conservation, economic activities, and community interests.
- **Reduces Risk:** Clarifies legal rights, reduces overlapping claims, and accelerates project permitting.
- **Supports Impact Measurement:** By mapping activities and outcomes, MSP helps monitor and report on progress toward sustainability and blue finance targets.
- **Informs Investment Decisions:** Investors and lenders can better assess risk, viability, and potential impact when ocean space is well-managed and transparently governed.

Synergies between Finance Plans and MSP

- **Integrated Approaches:** Aligning finance plans with MSP ensures that investment flows are matched to spatial priorities and ecological carrying capacities.
- **Adaptive Management:** Both tools support adaptive management, enabling course correction as new information, technologies, or stakeholder needs arise.
- **Data and Technology:** Advances in ocean mapping, remote sensing, and data platforms enhance both finance planning and MSP.

Institutional Arrangements

Establishing dedicated blue economy or ocean finance units within ministries, or inter-ministerial task forces, can enhance coordination and accountability. Legal and regulatory frameworks should mandate integration of finance and spatial planning.

Outcomes

When national ocean finance plans and MSP are developed and implemented together, countries are better equipped to attract investment, ensure environmental integrity, and deliver broad-based benefits to society.

Future Directions for Scaling and Mainstreaming Blue Finance

The future of blue finance lies in mainstreaming its principles, instruments, and impact into global and domestic capital markets, development agendas, and everyday decision-making. To meet the urgent needs of ocean health, climate resilience, and sustainable prosperity, the following trends and priorities are shaping the next wave of blue finance.

Mainstreaming in Global Capital Markets

- **Standardization:** The development and widespread adoption of taxonomies, reporting standards, and impact metrics will reduce transaction costs, enable aggregation, and build confidence for mainstream investors.
- **Liquidity and Secondary Markets:** As more blue bonds, loans, and structured products are issued, the development of liquid secondary markets will enhance exit options, price discovery, and market participation.
- **Integration with ESG and Climate Finance:** Blue finance will increasingly intersect with broader ESG, climate, and nature-positive finance initiatives, leveraging synergies and accessing larger pools of capital.

Innovation and Technology

- **Digital Platforms and Data:** Ongoing innovation in blockchain, AI, satellite monitoring, and big data analytics will improve transparency, verification, and efficiency, reducing barriers to entry for both projects and investors.
- **Financial Engineering:** The continued evolution of blended finance, insurance products, and impact-linked securities will enable more tailored and effective risk-return structures.

Enabling Ecosystems and Capacity

- **Capacity Building:** Investment in human capital, institutions, and local expertise will accelerate project pipeline development and ensure inclusive participation.
- **Partnerships:** Multisectoral partnerships, spanning government, private sector, NGOs, philanthropy, and academia, will be central to driving scale and innovation.
- **Policy Leadership:** Pioneering countries and regions will set the pace through ambitious policy frameworks, demonstration projects, and thought leadership.

Equity and Social Inclusion

- **Community-Driven Finance:** Models that empower Indigenous and local communities as co-investors, co-managers, and beneficiaries will become more common.
- **Gender and Youth Inclusion:** Blue finance will increasingly integrate gender and youth considerations, both as a matter of equity and as a pathway to unlocking innovation and social impact.

Climate and Nature Nexus

- **Scaling Blue Carbon:** Blue carbon markets and natural climate solutions will play a growing role in both voluntary and compliance carbon markets.
- **Nature-Positive Finance:** Mainstreaming biodiversity and ecosystem service outcomes will shift blue finance from "do no harm" to "net positive" impact.

Governance and Accountability

- **Monitoring and Enforcement:** The scaling of blue finance will require ongoing investment in governance, monitoring, and enforcement to maintain credibility and prevent blue-washing.
- **Learning and Adaptation:** Mechanisms for adaptive management, learning, and feedback will be built into all levels of blue finance.

Conclusion

The future of blue finance will be defined by innovation, integration, and inclusivity. As financial markets, policy frameworks, and civil society align behind the urgency of ocean action, blue finance is poised to move from niche to norm, driving transformative change for people, planet, and prosperity.

Conclusion

The oceans are the lifeblood of our planet. They regulate climate, provide food and livelihoods for billions, support global trade, and house much of the planet's biodiversity. Yet, as this book has demonstrated, the world's oceans and coasts face mounting pressures from overexploitation, pollution, climate change, and inadequate management. Addressing these challenges requires a step-change in ambition and a coordinated, well-financed global response. Blue finance stands at the center of this transformation.

From Margins to Mainstream: The Rise of Blue Finance

In the past decade, blue finance has evolved from a niche concept to a key pillar of global sustainability, climate, and development agendas. The growing recognition that healthy oceans underpin economic resilience and social wellbeing has catalyzed the development of innovative financial instruments, from blue bonds and debt-for-nature swaps to blended finance and tokenized blue assets. These tools are not only mobilizing new resources but are fundamentally reshaping how investments are structured, evaluated, and governed.

Crucially, blue finance is about more than just raising capital. It is about changing the relationship between finance and nature, embedding ESG considerations, impact measurement, and accountability into every stage of the investment cycle. It is about leveraging the power of public, private, and philanthropic actors to direct resources where they are most needed, supporting both the regeneration of marine ecosystems and the prosperity of coastal communities.

Key Achievements and Lessons Learned

The journey toward mainstreaming blue finance has brought important achievements and valuable lessons:

- **Innovation in Financial Instruments:** The development and deployment of blue bonds, results-based finance, and blended capital structures have created new pathways for mobilizing resources at scale. These instruments have proven their value in attracting diverse investors and aligning incentives with ocean-positive outcomes.
- **Enabling Policy and Governance:** The rise of national ocean finance plans, marine spatial planning, and clear regulatory frameworks has provided the structure and certainty needed to unlock both domestic and international investment. Harmonized taxonomies and reporting standards are increasing transparency and comparability.
- **Measurable Impact:** Advances in measurement frameworks, ranging from key performance indicators to rigorous ESG reporting and third-party verification, have improved the ability of investors, governments, and civil society to assess and compare impact. The focus has shifted from inputs and intentions to real-world outcomes for biodiversity, ecosystem services, livelihoods, and carbon.
- **Inclusivity and Equity:** The best blue finance initiatives are those that put local, Indigenous, and community voices at the center. Meaningful participation, benefit-sharing, and respect for traditional knowledge are not just ethical imperatives but drivers of effectiveness and sustainability.
- **Adaptive Learning:** Oceans are dynamic, and so too is the field of blue finance. The most resilient approaches are those that embrace adaptive management, continuous learning, and flexibility in the face of uncertainty.

Persistent Challenges and the Path Forward

Despite progress, the scaling of blue finance faces persistent challenges that demand continued attention:

111

- **Investment Gaps:** The gap between current investment levels and the funding required to achieve global ocean goals remains large. Project pipeline development, capacity building, and aggregation of small-scale projects are ongoing priorities.
- **Risk Perception:** Perceived and actual risks, regulatory, environmental, financial, and social, can limit private sector participation. Continued innovation in de-risking mechanisms, insurance, and blended finance is essential.
- **Governance and Enforcement:** Robust monitoring, transparency, and enforcement mechanisms are critical to maintaining market integrity and preventing "blue-washing." This includes ongoing harmonization of standards and investment in independent verification.
- **Data and Measurement:** Gaps in data and standardized metrics, especially for biodiversity and ecosystem services, must be addressed to support effective decision-making and reporting.
- **Equitable Access:** Ensuring that blue finance reaches the most vulnerable and empowers local actors is essential for legitimacy and impact. This includes targeted support for small island developing states, women, youth, and Indigenous peoples.

Opportunities for Transformation

Looking ahead, the blue finance landscape is rich with opportunity:

- **Digital Transformation:** Technology, including blockchain, big data, and digital monitoring platforms, will continue to increase transparency, efficiency, and participation, opening up blue finance to new investors and models.
- **Nature-Positive and Climate Solutions:** The convergence of blue finance with broader climate and nature-positive finance movements will accelerate investment in blue carbon, restoration, and ecosystem-based adaptation, offering powerful synergies with global climate goals.

- **Mainstreaming Blue in Global Markets:** As blue finance is integrated into mainstream ESG investing, capital markets, and policy frameworks, the potential for transformative scale increases exponentially.
- **Leadership and Partnerships:** Champions, whether countries, cities, companies, or community organizations, will continue to drive ambition, innovation, and collaboration, inspiring others and raising the bar for what is possible.

The Call to Action

Blue finance is not a silver bullet, but it is a cornerstone of a more resilient, inclusive, and sustainable future for the oceans and the billions who depend on them. Achieving the full potential of blue finance will require:

- Strong political will and leadership at all levels, from global institutions to local governments and communities.
- Continued innovation in instruments, governance, and measurement to keep pace with the changing nature of ocean challenges and opportunities.
- Deep, cross-sectoral partnerships that bridge finance, science, technology, and community expertise.
- A relentless commitment to transparency, accountability, and equity, ensuring that no one is left behind and that the true value of the ocean is recognized and protected.

As we look to the future, the task is clear: to scale blue finance not as a niche or afterthought, but as a core pillar of the world's response to climate, biodiversity, and development imperatives. By aligning financial flows with ocean health, we can unlock a sustainable blue economy that delivers prosperity, resilience, and regeneration for generations to come.

The time for ambition is now. The tools are at our disposal. What remains is to act, boldly, collaboratively, and with the long-term health of the ocean and humanity at heart.

www.ingramcontent.com/pod-product-compliance
Lightning Source LLC
Chambersburg PA
CBHW052139270326
41930CB00012B/2945